DANCES WITH DONKEYS

The Memoir Of A Half-Assed Cowboy

JIM DUKE

WILD BLUE
P R E S S

WildBluePress.com

DANCES WITH DONKEYS published by:

WILDBLUE PRESS
P.O. Box 102440
Denver, Colorado 80250

WILDBLUE PRESS is registered at the U.S. Patent and Trademark Offices.

ISBN 978-1-960332-05-9 Trade Paperback
ISBN 978-1-960332-07-3 eBook
ISBN 978-1-960332-06-6 Hardback

Interior Formatting and Cover Design by Elijah Toten
www.totencreative.com

DANCES WITH DONKEYS

Contents

Through the Looking Ass

"Why do you keep such ugly beasts?"
it's often asked of me.
"Why not have one horse at least,
so beautiful, wild, and free?"

It seems so plain, so obvious,
how could I feel ill-fated?
To surround myself with the very best
that ever were created.

A friendship now days known by few,
the very best companions.
Contented just to pack us through
the mountains, plains, and canyons.

It seems forever, more or less,
he's shouldered mankind's loads
and brought us through the wilderness
with little use for roads.

And while I'm no religious man,
it must show good behavior
to be chosen as delivery van
and guardian of the savior.

He provides us with solutions
for problems yet uncounted,
but his greatest contributions
are not when he is mounted.

When you gaze upon a grazing jack,
you may see a lowly ass.
You can be sure he's looking back
'neath the guise of nibbling grass.

He wears the perfect poker face,
he is what you impose.
But while you stand there heels in place,
he's always on his toes.

Unknowing eyes will think they feast
upon a silly creature.
A simple, strange, and awkward beast
without redeeming feature.

Those that are demanding
will find his every fault
and take each patient standing
as a personal assault.

If then they try to use some force
and find he can't be budged.
He's judged the wrong end of a horse,
themselves correctly judged.

But patient, understanding eyes
might find a lifelong friend,
one to trust when hard times rise,
one to count on to the end.

So, if you see a lowly ass,
then that's just what he'll be
when viewing nature's looking glass,
you are just what you see.

Introduction

I've always wanted to be a cowboy but felt that I was born in the wrong place and at the wrong time. Being raised in the suburbs of university towns was hardly conducive to finding my life on the range, but from an early age I always managed to find my way around to the horse crowd. From our family cabin near Allenspark, Colorado in the mountains of Boulder County, where we spent the long summers provided by the schedules of university professors, I wandered, as a pre-teen, to the local livery stable and hung around until I was finally put to work. By my junior high school years, I'd found my way to a Black Angus and Quarter Horse breeding farm on the outskirts of Iowa City, where I toughened up by bucking hay during the summer and feeding cattle and helping to break horses after school for the rest of the year.

The horses were all handraised, gentle, for the most part, and easy to get started under saddle. The owner would saddle and longe a horse until it calmed down and seemed controllable before having me climb on for some more longeing. Young horses are often longed, which is working them in a circle on a long lead (longe). As soon as they started longeing smoothly and stopping on command, we would take them out on a pasture, dallied up on a fairly short lead at first, and then riding loose. It was rare to have one buck, and those that did weren't much of a challenge to stay on. Young horses generally don't know how to buck very well. I was often out loping around with fairly good control within an hour or two of first having saddled the horse.

Although it was all very simple and easy, it made me feel like a rough and tough, experienced cowboy. I was certain that I was being used for my skill and competence. Having been to Larry Jo's kids' camp when I was still young enough to wet my saddle, and having talked my parents into a few riding lessons since then, I thought I was quite the expert. To my boss, however, I was merely someone dumb enough to do whatever he told me to, and young and athletic enough to probably not get hurt in the process. Overconfident ignorance became somewhat of a repeating theme that has led to many of the best adventures of my life.

Beyond work, I also tended to gravitate toward the farm crowd socially. My best friend/worst enemy alternately throughout high school was a farm kid named Jim Walker. Because we both had the first name Jim, we were always referred to as Duke and Walker, titles that, like our friendship, have lasted a lifetime. It was at his farm that I learned to hunt, pluck and butcher chickens, and ride pigs. The first animal to buck me off was a huge boar hog, which proved to be the toughest and most adventurous ride of my life. After sneaking up for a flying mount, you sat on the highest and widest point on the pig with absolutely nothing to hang onto. Upon falling off, you were guaranteed to land in pig shit which, to make matters worse, provided little traction as you tried to escape the angry boar. And once you'd managed to sail headfirst out of the pig pen, you had to quickly regain your feet to keep running before Walker's large father, who strongly disapproved of pig riding, discovered the cause of all his pigs squealing.

Texas

As a generally distracted and poor student, I eventually dropped out of high school and headed to Texas to pursue my cowboy dreams—and to provide my parents with a little of the well-deserved peace and quiet they couldn't enjoy while I was raising cane around town. My academically oriented parents actually encouraged me to drop out and leave, not because they didn't care, but because they knew it to be the only solution for any of us. And while my moving to Texas undoubtedly provided my folks with some well-deserved peace and quiet, it did little to help me settle down and grow up.

If part of the qualifications for being a cowboy involves being a social misfit, then I was at least partly qualified. While I'd always been somewhat socially awkward, trying to mingle with the Texas cowboy crowd as a longhaired, bearded Yankee confirmed this image. And the farther I got from Austin, a liberal stronghold even back in the seventies, the greater the contrast between myself and the surrounding society. When I started working on a ranch near Wallis, about forty miles west of Houston, I might as well have been from a different planet.

By that time, Walker had graduated from high school and had come down to Texas to check out the ranch life. While we both hired on with the same "ranch investment firm," he'd been assigned to a place near La Grange when

I was moved to Wallis, so I was mostly on my own. That was probably just as well because we tended to cause more commotion and get in more trouble when egging each other on in our mutual poor judgment.

The ranch consisted of a couple thousand acres along the Brazos River, small by the dry, rocky West Texas standards but huge by East Texas standards, where fertile farms and ranches were more often described in terms of scores, or maybe hundreds of acres. With white snowy egrets flying around or following the exotic-looking Brahman cattle on the upper pastures, and the dark, vine- and moss-covered live oak woodlands around the river bottom sloughs, filled with alligators, water moccasins, and alligator garfish, this was a wild new world to me. Still fresh from the cornfields of Iowa, I felt like I was in deepest, darkest Africa.

And as foreign as all this seemed to me, I apparently seemed even more foreign to all the local inhabitants. This small rural community rarely encountered Yankees even passing through, much less a long-haired hippie sort of Yankee who fancied himself to be a cowboy and who apparently planned to stay a while. To them I *was* from a different planet. A planet way to hell and gone up north called Ohio, or was it Idaho? No matter. Anything that far from Texas might as well have been in outer space.

My boss, a man named Benny Mize, was the pillar of the community. He was built like a pillar too; square and stout. His jaw was square and his hands were large, work-swollen blocks, each supporting five smaller pillars for fingers. He enjoyed extending his large, square hand out to me, palm up, to display some small treasure, maybe an arrowhead he'd just found or some sort of ranching artifact or curious fossil, whatever. He would then slowly close his hand as a slight smile creased his chiseled face in a challenge to try to remove this valuable item from his iron grip. He would keep his eyes locked on mine to reiterate the challenge as he slowly transferred the treasure into his front pocket before returning to work, usually building or repairing fence.

I lived in Wallis for a relatively short time and never realized how important the town, and especially Benny Mize, had been in my life, until forty years later when I received a text message from my sister, Peg, in Austin.

The text message simply said, *"Benny Mize died."*

"Benny Mize died." I can't remember the last time three words have had that much impact. The memories, emotions, and confusion all caught me by surprise. I couldn't remember the last time Benny had even crossed my mind and never realized what an important figure he'd been in my life. Benny Mize dead? It just didn't seem possible. People like that don't die. But then again, he was already ancient the last time I'd seen him some forty years ago. He must have been at least forty or fifty way back then. How could he still have been alive after all those years? But how could he be dead? I had the startling realization that I was much older than he'd been the last time I saw him. Another impossibility. I tried to visualize Benny as a frail old man but couldn't get it to register.

I called my sister to only further confuse the situation. "Benny's daughter had specifically requested that you be notified," Peg told me. "Apparently he still talked about you in his later years." I shamefully tried to remember that Benny had even had a daughter, just to distract myself from the fact that I'd remained in his life while I'd let him slip from mine. While it was immediately obvious how important he had been to me, it was beyond concept that I'd had any impact at all on that immovable mass of man. I thought again of his iron grip. Benny never released anything. What I wouldn't have given to have visited him just once in all those years.

Benny had lived in Wallis several miles from the ranch and managed several other ranch properties, so he would only show up intermittently. I lived alone on the two-thousand-some-odd-acre ranch in a house (ranch style, I guess) about a half mile past the locked gate on the highway. Although I'd lived only two hours away in College Station eight years earlier, that was several lifetimes ago to a twenty-year-old (ten years is just a glance over my shoulder at my current age) so I was basically a newcomer, fresh from Iowa. The Brazos River frontage, with its armadillos snuffling around in the dirt in their nearsighted way, sometimes right up to my feet, to look me up and down and maybe sniff a couple times before zipping away with amazing speed, the mockingbirds singing constantly, but never repeating themselves, the rattlesnakes on the high ground, the cottonmouths down in the slough by the river, and the slow, muddy river itself were more wild, exotic, adventurous, and dangerous than anything I'd ever seen, and I loved having it practically all to myself.

As deacon of the church, Benny went through the motions of trying to save me, mostly by just cordially inviting me to church, but he wasn't the type to impose his beliefs on others, except for work ethics under his employment. Hands in pockets were rewarded with a cuff to the head as a reminder that men must always have their hands out and ready to work or fight. Anyway, I could tell his heart wasn't really into getting me baptized. I preferred to think that he sort of liked me the way I was, heathen and all. But the rest of Wallis didn't seem to share this casual attitude and I could tell he was pressured to lure me into their clutches. They figured they had themselves a genuine heathen, which made me somewhat of a contemporary issue. Not to mention the fact that I'd migrated practically around the world to wind up in their little community indicating that I was looking for change, maybe a revelation even, and it was obviously providence. At the very least I was lost, lonely, and young enough to be easy pickins for salvation. At the bottom of it all, however, was just a very friendly community trying to welcome an awkward stranger the best way they knew how.

I'd been there a couple weeks and had met Benny's sidekick, James Steward, a semi-retired old rancher who also had a key to our gate (and every other gate in the county) and who took great pleasure in having a hippie friend to come harass. I'd also met Benny's brother-in-law, Shorty, another part-time employee with the only other key to the gate that I was aware of. So, I was surprised to see a car coming down the drive late one afternoon after work. Benny and James drove trucks and Shorty didn't drive due to a constant state of drunkenness.

I don't think they gave DWIs in that area in those days. Shorty had just about wrecked every vehicle he ever had access to, including tractors and such. He'd run himself over with a tractor just a year or so before I moved there. Well, I guess he hadn't really run over himself as the tractor wasn't really moving forward, but was digging itself down, lodged against the foundation of an old fallen farmhouse he'd run into. Shorty had managed to get dragged under a rear wheel as it dug itself down, yet somehow lived to walk haltingly and talk unhaltingly. As Benny's brother-in-law, Shorty was more of a social and religious obligation than he was an employee.

Anyhow, this was the first time I'd seen an unknown vehicle approach my ranch house. This wouldn't have been any kind of big deal except that I, having settled in and feeling comfortable with my situation, had decided to have my own little housewarming party and had just smoked a joint. I'm pretty sure it was the first time I'd ever smoked pot alone because I remember thinking of the old truism, "Drinking alone is the first sign of alcoholism." It made me feel deliciously old, wicked, and derelict—I was already developing adult problems and I couldn't even vote yet.

It's amazing how high one gets when alone and without the distraction of others to share one's joint with. This is especially true when one starts running around in a panic trying to make sure all one's weed is hidden and that one looks and acts fairly normal, or at least not high as a kite, when walking out to greet... who the hell was this anyway? Having spotted this vehicle almost a half mile away over the flat, treeless terrain of the upper pasture, I had an eternity to work myself up to a frenzy as the car slowly crawled down the long, rutted, muddy two-track lane.

Could it be Benny, or maybe James, in a borrowed car or riding with someone else? Or maybe just Shorty with a friend? That would be the easiest option because they would be too drunk to notice my condition. I desperately hoped this to be the case. As it inched closer, I saw that it was a fairly new Lincoln Continental. *That can't be good. No wonder they're going so slow. Who would ever try to drive a lowrider like that down a muddy lane like this?* My panic increased as the car got close enough to make out the silhouettes of many heads. It was full. Who were they? I considered heading out the back door toward the woods down by the river. No, I had to get ahold of myself. They might have already seen me too. I'm sure I was very flushed and almost hyperventilating as I walked off the porch to greet them, trying my best to look calm, even bored, with the situation.

The sedan was crammed full with the entire Wallis Baptist Youth Organization. They were all about my age, late teens to early twenties. They ranged in character from the virgin daughter of the car's owner, who had never even been as far away as Houston, to local cowboys, and even included an ex-junkie from Houston, who was evidently put in the position of emissary and possibly translator to help break the ice with their new northern, hippie pagan. He seemed to be put in the lead position, being the most likely to be able to relate to me. Looking at me, I'm sure they were all pretty thrilled to have found a soul so obviously lost and needing to be saved.

After a little bit of very awkward conversation led mostly by the junkie and mostly about how messed up he, too, (subtle about my obvious situation) had been before finding Jesus, the virgin driver tried a different tact, saying Benny had mentioned that my dogs knew lots of really neat tricks. That at least gave me a familiar routine; bang bang play dead, walk on hind legs, balance food on nose until told to toss and catch it, jump up on my shoulders and balance piggyback, frisbee (hippie) tricks, etc. My accidental chocolate Labradoodle (I'd been devastated seeing that pansy-assed black poodle hooked up to my prize yellow Lab, whose future litter had already made me wealthy in my dreams) was smart as a whip and picked up any trick I showed her. The way those folks were all way too inordinately impressed by this little show was about all I can remember from our impromptu little get together, which lasted eternally longer than had their initial approach down my lane, except that I'd also been cornered into accepting their invitation to the church's annual summer picnic the next week.

The picnic was pretty much a repeat of the WBYO (Wallis Baptist Youth Organization) visit at the ranch, except that it had lots of adults and good food and even some beer available. The beer was possibly an exception for my benefit (even though I was underage) as it was commented on more than once, usually in a joking fashion, and often in comparison to Lutheran picnics, where whiskey was apparently drunk from paper cups and soda cans rather than openly—they appeared very self-conscious about it. But I appeared to be main attraction and everyone wanted to see all the dog tricks and, again, seemed to be way overly impressed by them. It was like being in the circus. I was the freak show, my dogs the trained animal act.

I'm fairly sure that everyone there extended a personal invitation to please join them in church… maybe next Sunday? They also had Bible study and prayer meetings several times a week, in case I was interested. I couldn't help but notice that neither James Stewart nor Shorty were anywhere to be seen. James Stewart turned out to be no more a churchgoer than me while Shorty, although rarely sober enough to reach the church on Sunday mornings, claimed to be very religious and was especially grateful for God's forgiving nature.

James Stewart was quite the character, always trying to be out of line with what he assumed would be my liberal, Yankee sensitivities, usually having to do with racial slurs, which he knew made me uncomfortable, but able to respond to almost anything inappropriately and with the greatest shock factor. He knew (as everyone except maybe Shorty knew) that I was nowhere near the cowboy I claimed to be and tried to act like, but was much less inhibited than others in teasing me about it.

A typical conversation might go as follows:

"Howdy, Mr. Stewart, how you doing today?"

"Well, not worth a damn, Duke. Why just this morning, I went to fart, and damned if I didn't shit my britches! What you bin doing 'ere lately, Duke? You got any them heifers stump broke yet? We gone be working cattle 'ere pretty soon and we gone need a few stump broke heifers."

I had no idea what he was talking about but thought I would just bullshit my way through and figure it out as I went along. "No sir, Mr. Stewart. I've been working on it but haven't had much time here lately."

James Stewart dragged this line of conversation out intermittently for several weeks without ever cracking a grin before I finally figured out that "stump broke" involved heifers backing up to a stump for a little barnyard sodomy.

Shorty was a small guy, probably about forty, but looked at least a hundred. Since I was from up north, he assumed my brain was pretty much a blank slate and was eager to teach me everything he knew. He encouraged questions, telling me that was the best way to learn, and using the example of a person missing a finger. "The first thing you're gonna ask that person is 'did it hurt?' on account a you ain't never had a finger cut off, so you don't know." He also gave me lots of practical advice for everyday living, such as, "If you smoke a pipe, always take it out of your mouth before starting a fight. God O Mighty! Thought I was gonna choke to death!" He encouraged me to avoid alcohol and especially not to try to run a bar with the help of a beautiful young wife. "Them places is the devil's playground!"

I once gave him a ride to go see his mostly estranged wife. I was surprised to be introduced to a fairly attractive, middle-aged woman with very flirtatious eyes and mannerisms, knowing Shorty was oblivious. I was even more surprised to meet his son, a very handsome and athletic-looking, 240-pound sixteen-year-old of mixed race. Shorty appeared equally oblivious to the lack of resemblance, just another of many awkward little encounters I was starting to get used to.

Out of boredom, loneliness, and libido, I occasionally dropped in at the Hilltop Tavern located a ways out of town on a straight stretch of highway that appeared to be flat as a pool table (flatter than the pool table in the bar anyway) to the distant horizons in either direction. It was there one evening that I was trying, drunk and desperate, to hit on the barmaid, the only potentially sinful young woman in town who was close to my age. Her eyes were slightly crossed and might have outnumbered her real teeth—anything to avoid stump breaking heifers. To this day, I count my lucky stars to have been unsuccessful, but still have occasional nightmares anyway.

On that particular evening she'd asked, probably just to make conversation, but possibly as an employee of the bar, how old I was, to which I gave my rote answer: "Twenty-one." I'd forever looked much younger than I was, still occasionally being pulled over by cops who couldn't believe I was even sixteen, much less twenty, and so could never figure out how I ever got away with drinking in bars, which I'd done frequently for a couple years. I'd never had a fake

ID, or usually even a real one, for that matter. It probably had something to do with the fact that I was always alone, unusual for youngsters sneaking into bars, and maybe by virtue of my ridiculously youthful appearance itself. Folks might have figured that nobody looking so young would ever try to pass for twenty-one if they weren't, and they probably thought I must have some congenital condition they didn't want to embarrass me about in front of others. Whatever the reason, nobody ever "carded" me in those days.

On that particular evening, however, after having given my rote answer of, "Twenty-one," I puzzled for a moment and then asked, "What day is it anyway?"

"Tuesday," she replied.

"No, I mean, what is the date today?"

"June 4."

"Shit! I really am twenty-one, it's my birthday!"

The few people in the bar all stopped whatever they were doing and looked at me. I was thinking I would probably be seeing a few free drinks sent my way but instead, the bartender sauntered over and asked to see my driver's license, which as usual, I didn't have with me. He took my Lone Star longneck, set it behind the bar, and pointed at the door. Some party.

I made sure I'd found my driver's license before I ever went back to the Hilltop, but I never was able to generate much rewarding social interaction with anyone there. The only person who had much interest in me was some old cowboy who moved over next to me at the bar and seemed to want to talk but couldn't seem to figure out what he wanted to say. And he had a look of desperation in his eyes that brought to mind my efforts to flirt with the cross-eyed barmaid. I started to suspect that he was a very frustrated and ashamed homosexual ("closet gay" wasn't known terminology in those days), and he likely assumed that I, as a longhair, was one of those like-minded young men he'd heard about, and possibly the solution to his lifelong frustrated fantasies. Who knows?

Due to my young and lonely appearance, I'd been hit on more than my fair share in the bars of Austin, and I was a bit homophobic at that point in my life. At any rate, the old cowboy was pretty much a fixture at the bar and made it difficult to try to socialize with anyone else or even have a peaceful beer by myself. The Hilltop wasn't barrels of fun and laughter anyway, so it wasn't too hard to give up.

Sometime in the next couple weeks I must have gotten lonely—and horny—enough to accept one of my many invites to go to church. Everyone has heard about how wild preachers' daughters can be, and having been on a couple CYO (Christian Youth Organization) trips in high school (nothing to do with religion, just a free bus ride to ski at Lacrosse Wisconsin where hell does indeed freeze over), I'd witnessed how much wild action can go on with these good Christians. I would wager that, at least in those days, most young women lost their virginity on church sponsored excursions.

I'd seen a few beautiful "Southern belles" around town, but never in any sort of situation where a shy and insecure outsider like me could have ever even spoken to them. This was compounded by the fact that I had no intention of getting married and settling down, as was the normal and acceptable mode in this region, and so I carried the guilt and paranoia of someone just wanting to get laid. I assumed I was sufficiently transparent regardless of efforts to hide or disguise my illicit intentions that I might as well be carrying a neon sign over my head to advertise this.

Anyhow, I was desperate enough to go check out the church scene or, more specifically, the church girls. This turned out to be somewhat difficult with the entire church crowd all trying very hard to act like they weren't checking me out. While I tried to calm my paranoias, I could feel the tangible, subdued energies of expectation engulfing me from every direction. About a hundred hours into the service, the preacher, Jean Frank, was nearing the end of his sermon. I really hadn't paid attention to it while trying to sneak glances here and there at various young women, but the sermon had almost certainly been geared toward converting heathens. He paused to get everyone's (my) attention, launched his arms and face up to the heavens, and declared, "What a beautiful day for salvation."

He brought his hands and face back down, ever so slowly and silently for maximum effect, his eyes landing on mine, which immediately dropped down to inspect the tops of my boots. Long silence. "A beautiful day for salvation," he repeated. Slightly shorter silence. "Is there anyone among us wishing to cleanse their souls of sin?" Pause. "And open their hearts to Jesus?" Pause. "Then come forward and pray with me and ye shall be forgiven." Longest silence. First, one person, and then another went to the front of the church to kneel and pray with Jean Frank (presumably pre-planned "stooges" to help show me what to do and provide company for the act).

From their lower vantage point and with their backs to the rest of us, their voices weren't as loud and clear but some "forgive me," and "I have sinned," and "thank you, Jesus" phrases could be heard by the rest of us. I risked a glance up to see Jean Frank standing over their bowed heads with one hand on each, his eyes still on me. I quickly looked back at my boots.

"Anyone," he repeated more loudly. "Anyone at all?" Several more joined the prayers up front. More mumbling emerged from among them as Jean moved about, touching bowed heads. "Would anyone else like to join us? Anyone at all?" A few more stepped forward, started to pray. "Or maybe you would like to renew your commitment to the Lord and share your love with Jesus. Come forward and pray with us!" Jean bellowed. More folks moved forward.

I glanced around just enough to realize I was sitting alone in the pews, with everyone else up front praying. Jean was still staring at me and repeated in full volume now, "Anyone, anyone at all." As I sat there staring at my boots, wondering how long this standoff could last, I again considered the notion of eternity. Religion seemed to involve a lot of eternities.

They never did get me baptized. Benny never got involved in trying. But Benny did give me somewhat of a spiritual awakening, although he wasn't trying to. I don't remember him ever trying to give me any sort of advice or direction other than what was necessary for the job at hand. I really can't remember anything he said to me, but only his ways and how he accepted me as I was. And somehow in his quiet ways, he gave me a new faith in human nature and kindness. He became a keystone in my foundation of human understanding and the basic good in life in general. I miss him enough now to make up for the forty years I didn't miss him at all.

The ranch in Wallis had little use for horses. The pastures were all easily accessible by truck, and the wooded bottom lands were so dense with brush and vines that they were barely reachable on foot, much less on horseback. We had a few horses nonetheless, but these were so spoiled and abused by the inexperienced ranch owners that they had a strong distaste and distrust of all humans. The owners consisted of a partnership of several "city slicker" types, some of whom were ex-pro football players, who invested in ranch properties to fix up for resale. The horses were there largely for appearances and for the occasional pleasure of the owners and their children, none of whom knew anything about horses.

The macho-minded ex-ball players in particular tended to be very heavy-handed to the point of being abusive. At that time, I didn't know enough about horses to either earn their trust or to correct their behavior, so the few times I attempted to ride resulted in continuous conflict with the poor beasts and wasn't much fun for either of us. It probably didn't help that the first time I rode any of them was also the first time I tried peyote. Walker had come to visit and had brought some peyote that he'd come across somewhere.

Neither of us knew how to clean it properly, resulting in both of us getting even sicker than what's normal with peyote. I'm pretty sure that my horse, named Screwy Louie for his erratic behavior, had never been puked off of before. Puking is a very extreme and unusual behavior and wasn't well received. All in all, it wasn't a good first experience with peyote for any of us and I'm sure that the horses, as sensitive as they are to our own moods and energies, weren't much pleased with our company. First impressions with critters are even more important than with other humans.

The only good horse experience I had while working for that outfit was when I was "loaned" to another ranch for fall roundup. This operation had some good cowponies and experienced hands who knew how to care for them. Being the newcomer, Yankee, and a hippie, I was somewhere below the lowest rung of the ladder and was stuck with the last choice in horses. He was a scrawny little guy with hairy fetlocks and other characteristics of the original Spanish Barb breeds first introduced by Hernan Cortez in the sixteenth century, and the ancestors of the original wild (feral) mustangs. Initially disappointed at being stuck with so inglorious a mount, I soon developed the appropriate respect for that little guy. He had far more stamina than any of the larger horses and was barely beginning to break a sweat in the heat of the day while the other horses were thoroughly lathered. Although we did the widest sweep around the ranch and covered more ground than anyone else, he was still going strong long after the large, muscular Quarter Horses were played out to the point of stumbling along.

I've been partial to these smaller breeds ever since. These breeds were the backbone of the American West. These were the ponies that could withstand the rigors of long-distance travel over the rough country encountered on cattle drives. Even then, each cowboy required a string of about half a dozen horses to rotate through. Andy Adams's book, *The Log of a Cowboy*, does an excellent job of describing the value of such horses in the harsh conditions of a cattle drive. The book, first published in 1903, is considered by historians to be one of the most accurate first-hand accountings of an actual cattle drive.

I occasionally got over to La Grange to visit Walker and check out his ranch situation. At that time, La Grange was still home to the most famous whorehouse in the south. It pre-dated the American Civil War and was called the Chicken Ranch because during the post-war poverty years, they began accepting chickens as payments and eventually started raising chickens and eggs as a side business. ZZ Top wrote a fairly well-known song called "La Grange" about that whorehouse.

Walker and I always had big plans to visit that whorehouse and always came up with weak excuses, not wanting to admit that we were too chicken to go to the Chicken Ranch. It wound up getting closed down in 1973, before we could ever build up the courage to give it a try. It was a terribly ugly scene when some glory-seeking uppity reporter embarrassed local officials into reluctantly shutting down their proud historic landmark that was claimed to have entertained more politicians than had the state capital. The story hit the front pages of many national magazines. It hit national news again several months later, when the same reporter returned for a follow-up story and was severely beaten by the sheriff, apparently one of many elected officials invested in the business. While this fiasco did serve to bring fame and launch a successful career in news reporting, the good ol' boy network in Texas never did forgive that transgression.

Although we never made it to the Chicken Ranch (or at least never made it from the parking lot to the front door), we did visit a whorehouse south of the border. One of our wealthy bosses had a high dollar bird dog that he wanted to have bred to some champion bird dog located down close to the border. I volunteered for the trip and Walker couldn't help but tag along. After having dropped off the bitch in heat and having miraculously survived a thorough vehicle search near the border, we stashed our weed and stuff and ventured into Mexico.

Our experience was likely the same as with any young men in that situation and didn't get too interesting until we tried to drive back across the border. My beat-up old truck with two half-drunk cowboys was an obvious target for being searched. The border patrol officers brought their dog over to sniff for drugs and, upon smelling the bird dog's odor of being in heat all over the seat, the dog started going wild. Certain that my truck was about to be dismantled, I started trying to explain the situation to the border guard, but he merely laughed and said he could tell the difference. With the dog rendered ineffective, the manual search intensified, and I still worried about my truck being dismantled if they found seeds or other evidence.

Walker apparently didn't share my concerns and was feeling like a smartass. When a guard asked where we got the bale of hay in the pickup bed, Walker replied that we'd stolen it from a poor old cow. I could have punched him, but the guard merely ignored him and cut the bale open to search through the contents. An hour or so later, we were back on the road and trying to remember where we'd left our stash. Although we'd used condoms, we both dosed ourselves heavily with antibiotics from my brother-in-law's veterinary clinic when we got home.

That was our last trip to Mexico together and the last errand we did for our wealthy bosses. It turned out that our "city slicker" ranch owners were as crooked as suggested by their company name, Captain Credit Cattle Company, and the whole operation went broke with a couple owners even doing time behind bars. One summer in the heat and humidity of the Houston countryside was plenty enough for me, and I was glad to get back to work at my brother-in-law's ranch near Paige, Texas. While not nearly as humid as the Brazos river bottom near Wallis, the summers were still pretty brutal and I became migratory, feeding cattle during the winter when my help was most needed and heading north to work at a guest ranch in Colorado in the summers.

While I did enjoy ranch work and especially working cattle, branding, castrating, and vaccinating during spring and fall roundups, much of the time in between could be pretty lonely and boring. I was forced to face the fact that I wasn't the loner I'd always fancied myself to be and wanted to be, but was instead a very social type. The main factor leading me away from ranching, however, was the realization that horses, not cattle, were my true passion. Maybe if I'd worked on a big spread in West Texas or another area where most of the work was done from horseback, I would have remained a cowboy forever. As it was, I found myself drifting away from the ranching life and more toward the wrangling life—or anything that involved working with equines.

Meanwhile, I'd discovered a by-product of the cattle business that provided me with some contraband on my northern journeys.

Traveling Medicine Man

It was the fall of 1975 and cattle prices had hit a record low. One old cow with a bad eye sold at auction for five dollars. My brother-in-law, John, had framed the check rather than cash it. He also decided to hold onto his calf crop that year and try not to sell anything until prices came back, resulting in a doubling of the number of cattle we usually overwintered.

Normally, the hardy coastal Bermuda grass, along with a little winter rye grass seeded in the woodlands, would get the herd through the winter with minimal supplemental feeding. But the ranch was soon grubbed down and I was feeding hay every day and loading up several tons of cottonseed cake at the Elgin coop a couple times a week to further supplement their diet. But as every cloud has its silver lining, so did this one, although it was of little benefit to the average Texas rancher.

I'd come to discover that my brother-in-law's ranch was in the middle of prime psilocybin country and for several years had been taking my harvests up to share with my long-haired friends in the remote hills of Boulder County. Doubling of cow herds is also a doubling of cow turds that nurture the magic *caca de vaca hongos* (cow shit mushrooms). Furthermore, the overgrazing created a situation where mushrooms were the tallest feature in the field and easy to find. It didn't hurt that I dried the caps in the hay barn, inoculating all the feed with spores. After a good rainstorm, I could fill a pickup truck with mushrooms as fast as I could pick them. It would have been worth a fortune to a capitalist with connections, but the mere thought of profit would have so offended the spirits as to derail aspirations of enlightenment, much less possibilities of becoming a Carlos Castaneda type *brujo*. It never occurred to me that I was any sort of drug runner, but merely an aspiring medicine man.

There had always been plenty of mushrooms around, but never so abundant and easy to harvest. In the past, I would usually have to hunt for them a little. It was actually lots of fun—sort of like an Easter egg hunt, only enhanced. It took me a while to realize that my fingers, which would stain a dark purplish-black color from the spores, were absorbing the psychotropic alkaloids. It took a near catastrophe to make me realize this fact.

I often conducted my "Easter egg hunts" from the roof of the ranch truck. When feeding cattle by myself, I would put the truck in granny gear and climb into the bed to flake off hay while the driverless truck idled through open pastures. I applied the same practice to harvesting mushrooms. In normal years, the grass was high enough to hide the cow pies and their treasures. Sitting on the roof gave me a better angle to see down through the grass over a longer distance.

Psilocybin mushrooms are quite beautiful growing in the wild. I often dried especially nice clumps of them intact on the cow pie and even tried a variety of varnishes to try to preserve them as little gift ornaments. But they never looked as good dried out and few folks appreciated the beauty of an old cow turd on their desks or countertops.

One exceptionally magnificent spring day, I was harvesting mushrooms from the top of the truck, jumping down to pick and climbing back to the roof to search. Running ahead of the truck, I'd been struck by the incredible beauty of one particularly outstanding clump of mushrooms and was down on my hands and knees admiring them. I found myself transposed into this miniature scene, relaxing on the coastline of a cow pie in the shade of a mushroom palm tree, when I was abruptly slammed back to reality by a bump from the rear. If I hadn't been such a quick and nimble young ninja, I would have run over myself.

With the coming of the bluebonnets of spring, the Elgin coop started selling laying pullets and other poultry. Always a sucker for fuzzy little critters, I often bought a chick or two for company while hauling cottonseed cake. Before I knew it, I had a flock of several dozen. As spring rounded toward summer and the thermometer rounded toward 100 degrees, I started thinking about Colorado. I was driving an old 1965 Rambler American sedan in those days but didn't want to leave all my poultry behind. I was also planning on taking as many mushrooms as I could fit under and behind my back seat.

The brilliance struck me like a thunderbolt! If I had all those birds in the back seat, nobody would ever dig through all that chicken shit to search me! They wouldn't even be able to get in and try unless they had some place to put all my birds. They couldn't just let them loose on the roadside, could they?

This wouldn't be my first time pushing the limits while hauling critters from Texas to Colorado. A few years earlier, a friend had shot a skunk before discovering six kits in a nearby den. I'd adopted them and tried to smuggle them on a flight from Austin to Denver. While long before all the scanning and searching, I was caught bottle-feeding them by a stewardess who decided the only logical thing to do was to ignore the situation. What would they do with me and who would take care of the babies?

At least on this trip, I would be in my own vehicle. The next day, I taped and stapled a fishnet from the ceiling to the top of my front seat to contain my birds in the back seat and headed to Colorado with thirty-five hens, one rooster, four ducks, two geese, and one turkey in the back seat, which was covered with a few layers of newspaper topped with old carpet, concealing uncounted volumes of mushrooms. My pet raccoon rode up front with me. The raccoon actually went back and forth under the seat, which was OK because she'd grown up with the chickens and got along well with them. That was a good thing because as smart as coons are, they're absolutely untrainable.

It didn't take long for all the birds to get cranky in the cramped quarters and start getting tangled in the fishnet trying to escape the geese, who were bullying everyone else. I soon had to pull down the fishnet to let the chickens spread out along the top of the seat. At a gas station in Central Texas, the service guy (they didn't have self-serve in those days) started eyeing my birds, acting as though a carload of poultry was commonplace, like maybe I was a traveling chicken salesman.

"That a game cock?" he asked.

"No, it's an Araucana," I replied.

He studied the rooster a while longer with a seasoned eye. "Looks game to me... Gitcher windshield?"

"Uh, yeah, sure. Thanks"

He squeegeed the windshield and then studied the bird some more. "He's game, awright." I didn't respond. He kept looking. "How much ya want fer 'im?"

"He's not for sale."

He kept looking. "You shore? Looks a might crowded in thar."

About then, my raccoon woke up and crawled up on the seat.

"Damn! Don't he eat them chickens?"

"It's a she and no, she doesn't eat the chickens."

"How'd ya train 'er not to eat 'em?"

"I didn't. She just doesn't eat them. They're friends."

"Damn! If 'at don't beat all! You shore ya don't wanna sell that fighting' cock?"

"He's an Araucana and he's not for sale."

"Check yer oil?"

"No, I'm good. See you later."

Although I'd planned on driving through the night, I found this trip to be especially tiring. This was made worse by my turkey, the most affectionate of the flock, who had been perched right by my shoulder trying to remain aloof from the fray. The pool sharks of the flock, turkeys don't scratch nervously about, pecking at anything and everything. They take their time, moving slowly and deliberately, picking their shots carefully. After dark, this guy was especially interested in the little blue light on the dash that flashed on whenever I hit the brights. He moved down to sit beside me and the next time I hit the brights, he was on it in a flash and pecked out the blue filter covering the bright bulb behind. Without the blue filter, the little bulb was so bright as to night blind me to outside lights and make driving difficult. I found little pieces of paper to fold up and stick in the slot to dim the light, but every time I hit the brights, the turkey appeared out of nowhere and struck again.

Exhausted and night blind, I finally pulled off in a roadside park and tried to sleep for a while. Every time a truck approached in the distance, my rooster thought it was the sunrise and crowed. It's amazing how loud that is in the confines of a small car, and I soon regretted not having sold him two gas stations ago. To make matters worse, although the chickens seemed to naturally face forward while moving down the road, they turned randomly when sitting still, and chickens apparently don't stop shitting just because they're asleep. My nap didn't last long and I was soon back on the road with a good supply of paper wads to stick in the bright/ dim slot.

While smoking on the job is probably not a recommended activity for drug runners, I'd rolled a joint to celebrate the sunrise as I often did on long trips. That particular morning, I was going over Raton Pass in a heavy fog. The fog was dense enough that I obviously wouldn't see the sunrise, but I took a few hits anyway. As I got stoned, the fog kept getting thicker. Soon I was bent over the steering wheel, straining to see the road and creeping down the interstate at about fifteen or twenty miles per hour. Suddenly, a semi-truck came barreling past me at full speed. I jerked back and looked in the rearview mirror, where I could see perfectly. The fog had built up a thick condensation on my windshield. I turned on the wipers and could see just fine. Realizing how lucky it was to have been a trucker instead of a trooper, I suffered a paranoid panic attack, questioning everything I was doing. Struggling through a non-existent fog seemed a far cry from enlightenment. Suddenly, everything seemed so absurd! The fighting cock, the turkey, the 'shrooms... I wished I could disappear back into the fog. But it didn't last long. Another toke and on down the road.

Several hours later, I pulled through Allenspark, Colorado right in the middle of their Bicentennial celebration, where I stopped to show off my poultry and pass out 'shrooms to everyone. It was likely the best non-combustible Fourth of July celebration in Allenspark history. It left a strong enough impression that old timers, to this day, greet my arrival in Allenspark with, "Packin' any poultry?"

Introduction to Asses

Ever since my earliest memories, I'd always wanted a horse and constantly pleaded with my parents to make this happen. Being raised in the suburbs of university towns by a chemistry professor father and a math tutor mother made this a very unlikely scenario. One day, much to my surprise, my father responded to my pestering by saying he would consider buying me a riding animal if I would consider a donkey or a mule rather than a horse. Now, although my dad had been raised in a small farm town in South Dakota, he hadn't been much involved with agriculture and seemed to have little interest in animals. There's no doubt he was encouraging this choice for my safety and for a more affordable critter to maintain, but how he would have known asses to be safer or more maintenance free is beyond me. No doubt my father was aware of and tried to explain to me the many advantages of mules over horses and no doubt I considered myself, even at age ten, to be way too knowledgeable to listen to such an egghead intellectual type and had to learn it on my own over the next several decades.

Being willing to accept a donkey as a last resort, I went with my dad to look at a white donkey he'd seen advertised in the paper. Our search took us over to the wrong side of the tracks to a neighborhood largely fenced in with junk cars, tractors, and various discarded household appliances, strung across with occasional barbed wire ("bob war" in cowboy lingo) and bailing wire in what is a familiar scene to most low-end mule traders. As is usually the case, this improvised fencing proved to be a much greater obstacle to all of us would-be cowboys than to the donkey, who seemed to enjoy thwarting us through this obstacle course around the neighborhood. While obviously free to go wherever he pleased, he never went far away and continually put himself in what appeared to be escape-proof corners just to keep our attention. After everyone but the donkey was played out, the owner set about convincing my dad about how gentle he was once caught and said he would call us when that happened. That was my only experience with asses until ten or twelve years later.

It was when I was working as a wrangler at Lane Guest Ranch in Allenspark that my veterinarian/rancher brother-in-law in Austin called to inform me that he'd had just come to own a fine breeding jack and if I could come up with some brood mares, we would be in the mule business. The owner of the guest ranch was a nice guy and a heavy drinker, so it wasn't hard finding him in the right frame of mind to negotiate some mule breeding out of the four mares he had in his dude string. I was soon headed for Texas to meet my new breeding jack.

Some Advantages of Mules

Mules are considered to be a prime example of hybrid vigor, displaying the best combination of both parents, especially the survival instincts, toughness, and endurance of the ass. Asses are basically the "camels" of the equine realm, commonly going days at a time without water in our most extreme deserts and then drinking up to 40% of their own body weight in one standing. They're also what equestrians refer to as "easy keepers," meaning they don't require nearly as much feed as a horse or pony of equal size.

The wild type survival instincts prevent asses and mules from spooking and running off cliffs or through fences and other dangers. This is why only mules are allowed in the Grand Canyon. A well-trained horse will jump off a cliff on command and could easily spook off one while a mule couldn't be forced to do so. Mules are also less prone to over-reacting and exacerbating situations like getting tangled in wire or rope, which could result in worse cuts or strangulation. They tend to be calmer and able to think things through rather than freaking out and further endangering themselves and others around them. They're also much less prone to run themselves to death, drink too much when overheated, eat too much, or many other things that horses are more subject to. Many old army veterans from when they still had mule corps would swear that mules have a sixth sense for danger and saved lives by refusing to enter mine fields or other dangerous situations. Old cowboys and trappers had many similar stories. The basic rule of thumb is that if you stick with your mule, you'll be OK.

Mules also tend to be generally much tougher than horses. Their hooves are often resistant enough that they don't require shoes in even the rockiest situations, and they're less prone to saddle sores, rope burns, and wire cuts. Early pioneers almost always rode mules because horses couldn't withstand the strenuous conditions of crossing the Great Plains without supplemental feed. Famed mountain man and U.S. Army General Kit Carson always rode mules. In 1976, there was a 3,500-mile horse race coast to coast across the U.S. called the Great American Horse Race, attracting the best endurance horses from around the world. While this type of contest is usually won by a well-bred Arabian or Appaloosa, this particular race was won, easily, by a mule named Lord Fauntleroy.

Joshua T. Walker

As it turned out, my new breeding jack had been collected against one of those kinds of bad debts that get worse when they're collected on. And I could call him "my" jack because my brother-in-law had already soured on our partnership. Like the white ghost ass of my distant past, Joshua was pretty much on his own agenda and had been offered mostly because he couldn't be caught. Joshua also had that little bit of extra spirit that comes with a set of testicles. I'll never know what my brother-in-law went through to get Joshua caught and hauled home. He really didn't want to talk too much about it as he was still rationalizing his losses.

The first time I met Joshua, he was secured in a six-foot high board fence out back of my brother-in-law's vet clinic. Carefully latching the gate behind my two dogs and myself in response to the many warnings and threats about my fate if that "little sombitch" got loose again, I was immediately surprised when that "little sombitch" popped up, literally right out of the ground, and came at us with ears back, teeth bared, and hooves striking. His attack would have impressed the bravest of warriors, and I was about to turn and run smack into the gate when I realized he was only after the dogs. The dogs were quick enough to dodge his assault long enough for me to get them back out the gate.

I've since learned that, although they can be habituated and become friends with dogs, asses instinctively attack canines and most other predators. A young jenny imprinted on a flock of sheep or goats provides even better protection than the widely reputed Great White Pyrenees or other sheep dogs. Mules and asses have been known to fight off mountain lions and I know of one case where a miniature donkey fought off a black bear far larger than itself, although not without significant vet bills in the aftermath.

After removing my dogs from the pen, I went to inspect the hole from which Joshua had initially appeared. The ground was soft sand and he'd dug a pit large enough for him to walk down and disappear into in an effort to dig out under the fence. It looked like he might have had trouble with the concept of digging back up to the surface on the other side or he would have been gone.

Not having any stock rack for my truck, I set about building one out of some scrap wood I scrounged here, there, and yonder. The end result might not have been the most impressive piece of work, but I was on a tight schedule getting back to my wrangling job in Colorado and figured it would suffice for one little burro. When I rounded up my brother-in-law, John, to help get Joshua loaded, he took one look at my rack, said, "That ain't gonna hold shit!" and whacked the top rail with the heel of his hand in what a martial artist might call a palm thrust, thus breaking out said rail. Now, bear in mind that John is a large man and used to be an all-American football star for the University of Texas. Some years earlier I had, at his request, built a small cover for an electrical box on a power pole in a cow pasture on his farm. He'd taken one look at it, said, "That ain't gonna hold shit!" and whacked one of the boards off with the same sort of palm thrust. Now, some thirty years later, having been used as a backscratcher by fifteen generations of cattle, the same box still stands intact missing only the one board.

At any rate, his unwelcome critique didn't result in any vast improvements as it had already been tough finding full eight-foot lengths of scrap when it had been daylight and since it was getting late and I was raring to go, I just scabbed on another short piece with bailing wire. As previously mentioned, John had already started to sour on this mule-breeding business before I'd even shown up and didn't seem to be getting any more optimistic as we went along. He didn't seem to have any strong affection for Joshua at that point, but neither did he want to see him dropped out of a high-speed truck or possibly land on someone else's car. On the other hand, it was getting well past his bedtime, and he was more than ready to be rid of all the jackasses involved in this project. Thus, he decided that an appropriate dose of sedative, acepromazine, I believe, would keep Joshua sufficiently calm that he wouldn't test the rack.

This task required a twitch (a device to pinch the upper lip), a Scotch hobble (a rope holding a hind leg off the ground), and a blindfold to hold Joshua still enough for an intravenous injection and, as soon as we got him in the truck, he started staggering around like two drunks trying to carry a barrel between them—the front end didn't seem to know what the back end was doing or vice versa. Bouncing off the sides of my rack while I tried to wire up a half-assed tailgate, Joshua managed to knock loose the spare tire I'd wired up on the inside of the rack and then kick a hind hoof through the center hole of it. Well, it turns out that the center hole of a half-ton Ford truck wheel is almost the exact same size as an average donkey hoof. It also turns out that the center hole is punched out such that it's rounded and smooth on one side (the side through which Joshua's hoof entered the wheel) with a squared off, somewhat sharp edge on the other side, giving it more resistance one direction that the other with the same principle employed by fishhooks, porcupine quills, and other hard-to-remove items.

Now, for those readers who are totally appalled by my stupidity and the potentially disastrous results, I must concede that any animal handler should be ashamed of such an incident, but no injury resulted from this blunder. This in itself bears testimony to the toughness and survival instincts of *Equus asinus*. Any horse in a similar situation would have blown up and either struggled itself to death or injured the fetlock so severely as to necessitate euthanasia. In this case, however, without even scratching the soft skin of his fetlock, Joshua just banged the tire around the back of the truck long enough to finish waking up whatever neighbors had managed to sleep through John's shouting and cussing and then, realizing his predicament, showed his first sign of submission, holding still to let us help him. Even with his cooperation, however, it proved necessary to further sedate him and put him completely under in order to whittle down his hoof enough to fit back through the center hole of the wheel. John, who was still learning about an ass's resistance to drugs, mumbled something about having given him enough to kill three horses and said he should stay unconscious for quite a while.

And so began my education as I headed for Colorado with an unconscious breeding jack who was on his feet and stumbling around again before I even hit the interstate. Fortunately, he settled down pretty quick with his butt braced against the rack hard enough to bow out the bottom rail, allowing him a little seat on the edge of the pickup bed. I don't think he moved the whole trip except possibly to relieve himself when the truck was stopped, and then again on the final mile of dirt road leading to the dude ranch. Along this last stretch, he seemed to realize that this was the place he ought to get out and, accordingly, stood up and stepped forward to slack off his halter rope enough to turn his head and look around. This also put enough slack into his halter (which was a horse halter and way too big for him) to allow him to slip it off somewhere along the last several hundred yards.

We pulled up to the stable just as a group of ranch guests were gathering for a ride, while a couple other wranglers brought the last few horses out to the hitching rail. Just as the truck reached a full stop, Joshua spun around to the rear and made a wild leap, easily snapping the half-assed wooden rails I'd wired across the rear of my rack as he sailed over the tailgate. Hitting the ground on the run, he appeared to be wide awake, perky, and well recovered from any sedation as he beelined it to the hitching rail, snapping reins as he bucked and kicked along between the horses and the rail as if he'd been there all his life and had it all planned out. Many horses tend to find burros to be pretty spooky critters at best, and this sort of introduction was nowhere near the best. As the horses spooked every which way, Joshua made one quick lap around the guests, tack room, and corral, taking the time to duck under the bottom rail into the corral and try to chase as many of the remaining unsaddled horses through or over the fence as he could before ducking back under in a different spot to round up his new herd and head up the nearest trail.

Needless to say, that ride was canceled while the other two wranglers and I mounted the few remaining horses to recover the loose ones. My two wrangler buddies, Scott and Frank, got a real kick out of the whole deal, and even the guests seemed to appreciate the show more than they would have the ride. Funny thing about dude ranch guests—the more you inconvenience them, make them miserable, or scare them without any real harm being done, the more they seem to enjoy the whole deal afterward, the more they have to talk about at the bar that night, and the bigger the tips.

Anyhow, Joshua started out with a very bad but popular reputation which just kept getting more notorious. I kept making every mistake in the book and he kept taking advantage of every opportunity thus offered. The next day, we decided to go ahead and break him to ride since he appeared to be sufficiently stout and energetic and might as well earn his keep while waiting to be a breeding jack. Now Scott, Frank, and I all thought we were pretty hotshot horsemen and had all had at least a little exposure to breaking and training horses, but we seemed to interact in a way that made us collectively clueless.

Frank was a stout fellow and offered to hold Joshua while I got on. None of the saddles fit too well and we weren't aware of the importance of a britchen or crupper on asses, due to their lack of withers (the ridge between their shoulder blades) like horses have. This lack of withers allows saddles to slip forward over their necks. Quite a few of the guests had started gathering to watch, which was fine with us as we were all anxious to prove what rough and tough cowboys we were and got pretty competitive in our efforts to show off. Frank held the struggling Joshua short while I gently swung into the saddle.

While I guess we hadn't discussed any specific plan, I'd assumed Frank would slowly play out a little line and longe Joshua around in a fairly tight circle. Whether by ignorance or accident, that's not the way it turned out. Before I even got seated, Joshua had jerked the rope out of Frank's right hand, in response to which Frank dropped all the slack and wrapped the tail end of the rope around his butt to brace for Joshua hitting the end of the rope. Joshua, with about fifteen feet of slack rope on the ground, took a dead run straight away from Frank. Running with his head down as wild asses generally do when trying to shed a load, Joshua hit the end of the rope, nearly flipping himself over while launching the stout Frank ten or twelve feet onto his face.

Although I managed to stay in the saddle, the saddle didn't stay on Joshua and at the first jolt slid right over his neck for lack of a crupper, landing me right in the path of his forward roll. With catlike agility, Joshua managed to put a half twist into his roll, turning it into more of a "round off," allowing him to land on his feet facing the direction he'd come from, and directly on top of me. That was the first of several times I've been shown an ass's belly, but I've never yet been stepped on. They seem to be pretty careful about that, their hooves preferring solid ground to squishy humans. With all three wranglers on the ground (Scott had fallen down laughing so hard), Joshua finished slipping the saddle over his head and, carefully stepping clear of it, took off running, dragging Frank along on his stomach a ways before he got untangled from the rope.

Before trying again, I rigged up a britchin from a pack saddle and cleared out the corral to use as a breaking pen rather than putting Joshua on a longe line. This time, he ran and ducked and crow hopped a little, and then discovered he couldn't duck the fence with a saddle on, but he didn't seem to know much about bucking and settled down fairly quickly.

Never having been very patient about training animals, I've always rationalized "on the job training" as an excuse to be running around totally out of control. Thus, we went on our first trail ride that same day with an extra wrangler along to try to stay between and protect the guest riders from Joshua and me. We occasionally took the lead out front as unbroken asses tend to drive better than lead and don't like to be approached from the rear, and sometimes followed. I had very little control over Joshua and his efforts to harass any horse he could get close to, trying to get either of us kicked as he seemed to enjoy a good kick over a dull ride, but most of the time we were off to one side or the other crashing through timber, sliding down talus fields (he soon learned his tremendous advantage on downhill stretches), or negotiating whatever other obstacles appeared most challenging to him that day.

Although there aren't too many thorn-bearing plants in the high alpine, Joshua usually managed to find at least a patch of wild roses or a dry, south-facing hillside with lots of thick, scraggly oak brush, rocky outcrops, and a few prickly pear cacti. He also really enjoyed thick lodgepole stands or quaking aspen groves with lots of downed timber because anything he couldn't duck under, he could jump over, often leaving me to the last second trying to figure out which course it would be. These jumping and ducking courses also had the advantage of often whacking my toes or shins, which hung below his belly (he stood just a little over twelve hands), into many of the logs that he barely cleared. Thankfully, asses have an instinctive fear of boggy areas, but Joshua occasionally managed to swallow his own fear to give me the thrill of careening through beaver colonies, where the chewed off willow stubs looked like jungle warfare death pits of sharp spears interspersed with hidden holes, tunnels, and soft, boggy spots.

One of Joshua's most impressive feats involved his first encounter with a cattle guard. During a peaceful and apparently too boring ride down Cabin Creek Road, Joshua took a sudden, high-speed detour down a private drive leading to a cute little cabin with a meticulously manicured lawn full of beautiful flowers with raised beds, hanging pots and rose arbors and such. So great was the owners' pride and investment in this elaborate landscape that they'd installed a twelve-foot-wide cattle guard to assure that no livestock could ever desecrate their efforts.

Approaching at a dead run, I braced myself for whatever tricky turn, dodge, stop, or miraculous maneuver Josh had in mind, confident that his distrust of man-made objects would force him to do anything except step onto that cattle guard. But before I could react, and to my amazement, he did the most incredible, high speed, tiptoe tap dance across the cattle guard, seemingly hitting every cross member without ever missing a step.

Two high speed laps around this cute little cabin with flowerpots, bird feeders, and wind chimes flying in every direction convinced Joshua that the only way out was the way he'd come in and again, before I could react, we were bearing down on the cattle guard at full speed.

Certain that he couldn't pull off his tap dance a second time, I pulled my feet from the stirrups, hoping to survive the wreck that was sure to cause him fatal injuries. Sticking with him till the last second, trying desperately to stop or turn him, I braced both hands on the saddle horn, hoping to launch myself, handspring style, clear of the inevitable tumble. This time, however, instead of the tap dance, I found myself flying through the air as he made a wild leap across the cattle guard, clearing the twelve-foot span with a foot or two to spare. Having prepared to launch off the saddle with my hands on the saddle horn is the only thing that allowed me to hang on and land back in my saddle upon touchdown. Our string of twelve riders was still passing the driveway on their peaceful ride as Joshua and I returned to the end of the line.

Joshua just kept getting more spoiled in every way, learning every trick in the book on how to cause the most commotion with the least effort, becoming somewhat of a symbol of manhood and mark of machismo for those willing to try riding him. Though the continual circus act was a lot of fun, even from the receiving end, and getting lots of attention merely for doing everything wrong probably didn't help the situation, Joshua was never intentionally taught bad habits. I truly wanted him to be a well-trained, handy, and of course, show off-able animal, but I just kept making one mistake after another. All the reverse training on Joshua was due to pure ignorance piled on top of the best of intentions. I made every effort to buddy up and gain his trust.

Several times, I took Joshua out camping by ourselves in hopes that he would get lonely enough to accept my company. Sleeping at the foot of the tree he was tethered to, hoping he might buddy up, I was lucky never to have been strangled by his tether (something he once nearly accomplished on a loose horse), but never occasioned anything more serious than having Joshua crap right inside both my boots, which is all the more remarkable because I could swear I'd laid them down sideways, as always when camping, to keep the dew out. We did eventually come to a somewhat intermittent, but workable truce that allowed me to even get away with riding bareback occasionally—if I was feeling exceptionally bold and adventurous and there was the right crowd of pretty girls to be impressed.

A typical morning might go something like this: Joshua would sing his heart out just before sunrise, waking most people for several miles. We wranglers would head down to check on and feed the animals before we ate, so they would have plenty of time to fill up before a hard day's work. I would walk over to get Joshua's water bucket where he'd dropped it on the far side of the tree he was tethered to, because no fence on the place could hold him. Joshua would shy away to the farthest point of his tether before stepping forward to slowly, curiously, walk halfway around me as I stood by the bucket talking to him and reassuring him that I was his friend. Then, as I would bend over to pick up the bucket, he would use this motion as an excuse to spook and rear back, snapping against the end of his tether. Seeing his motion from the corner of my eye and realizing too late that I was about to get closelined by Joshua's tether, I would make a desperate leap, trying to clear the rope as it swept under me. Not having jumped in time, the rope would catch my ankles and throw me into a sprawling layout back flip, slamming me down on my stomach and reminding me, once again, how it helps to exhale completely before having the shit knocked out of you.

This would leave Scott, once again, rolling around in the dirt laughing uncontrollably regardless of the clean, bright, and fancy, freshly pressed shirts and kerchiefs he liked to wear in the fashion common to dude ranch cowboys. Scott sure had to do a lot of laundry that summer, but I'd never seen a happier cowboy.

A favorite activity I had with Joshua was to pass myself off as a highly skilled tracker, claiming that I could judge the age of a track practically to the minute and could always pick out the freshest trail, even at a dead run. After making enough outrageous claims to ensure I would be challenged,

I would place a bet that however many wanted to take my wager could mount up and have a half hour's head start (enough to pass several forks on well-traveled trails) and I would be able to track them down within the hour. Then, to give them still a better advantage, I would even do it on Joshua. Little known to anyone else, Joshua had a nose like a bloodhound and loved tracking down any member of what he considered to be "his herd," especially the mares, which I always included in the parties to be tracked down. Another thing most folks didn't realize was that donkeys (particularly jacks chasing jennies or mares) have much greater stamina than horses, especially in the rougher steep mountain terrain. Consequently, the horses, and even more so their "holiday horsemen" riders, would start to play out pretty quickly after fifteen or twenty minutes of trotting or loping.

Joshua absolutely thrived on these "hide and seek" outings and, without even trying to get rid of me, would bray once or twice, either in an effort to call his herd back together or to shout, "Ready or not, here I come" (I was never sure which), and then put his nose to the trail and take off at a good clip that he would keep up until all the horses were accounted for. At any fork in the trail, he would usually make the right choice first try, but if not, he would quickly correct himself and get back on the trail.

I'd planned on entering the Get Your Ass Over the Pass race in Leadville, Colorado. This is a very well-known donkey race requiring the racer to run with the donkey rather than ride it. It's a grueling, marathon-length race over a high mountain pass. I was a fair distance runner in those days but was counting on Joshua to pull me along, pursuing the trail of the mare I planned to have someone ride across the pass the day before the race. Probably just as well that I didn't get around to it that year because the race organizers were wise to that scam and someone else got busted for trying the same plan.

Even though we kept him tethered most of the time, Joshua managed to escape on several occasions and once disappeared for over a week. Tracking him up into Rocky Mountain National Park and asking hikers I passed if they'd seen him, I heard some pretty harrowing stories, scary enough that I quit asking about him because I wasn't sure I wanted to be associated with him. The worst of these tales was from a hiker who said he'd been passed by a string of dude horses with guests from another local guest ranch. He said that about an hour later, he saw a donkey running up the trail with his nose to the ground and not long after that, the string of horses came running back down the trail without their riders, hotly pursued by the donkey. Hopefully, the guests had all been dismounted and having lunch or something when Joshua showed up, but I never found out for sure.

It was about a week later that I heard about "a cute little burro" showing up at the Peaceful Valley livery some thirty miles away. I cautiously approached the livery, fishing around with idle conversation for any wild tales or damage before trying to claim him.

Mule Breeding

As far as I know, Joshua never did any serious damage in his free-range rompings. But I suffered weeks of anxiety waiting to hear from someone seriously injured or worse from his exploits. While it eventually began to appear that he hadn't done any real harm during his escapades, neither had he done anything very worthwhile at home. In other words, we didn't seem to be getting any mares bred.

But then again, other than putting him in with the mares when they were cycling, we hadn't put much effort into it. The obvious problem was their difference in size, giving the appearance that Joshua would be very challenged in reaching any average-size mare. But all my old timer horse connections assured me that this was no problem and that jacks always seem to get the job done. We discussed digging a hole to stand the mares in and joked about some sort of elevator shoes for Joshua but ultimately, we let nature take its course. My hopes were dwindling as the mares kept coming back into heat, but I still clung to the hope of a late breeding as we put them all out to pasture for the winter.

I kept Joshua with me for the winter, rather than pasturing him with all the dude ranch horses, and I bought a mare and a molly mule that fall hoping Joshua might have better luck with this mare. I was really only interested in the mare to have as a brood mare, but they were offered as a pair for less than half the going price for even an unbroken horse, which she was, to say the least. She wasn't only not broke, but antisocial to the point of bordering on just plain mean. The first time I tried to catch her and had her cornered, she literally ran backward at me, kicking every other step.

Most of my critters, back in those days, came into my possession either cheap or free because they were either too wild or too mean for anyone else to deal with. That was fine with me because I fancied myself a rough and tumble sort, always ready for a challenge. I also thought it was cool to have a "one-man horse" (or ass) that no one else could handle. Bottom line, though, is that she and others from that period in my life, which unfortunately lasted decades, were just flat out dangerous. I was lucky to have survived and even luckier not to have seriously injured anyone else.

The molly mule, however, who was almost certainly a hinny (horse father, donkey mother) rather than a mule (donkey father, horse mother), turned out to be one of the greatest treasures and best friends of my life. She was, fortunately and unlike many mules, very forgiving, tolerated my heavy-handed, ill-tempered approach to equines, and taught me the value of kindness and patience, finally making a passable trainer out of me. Before I became aware enough to develop the appropriate level of respect for her, I'd already named her Fart Blossom, which stuck with her for the next thirty-seven years, my longest relationship on this planet.

Based on learning from mistakes, I learned a lot from Joshua, but all the most important things I learned about critters, including myself, came from Blossom. One of the more tangible things I learned through Joshua, indirectly from victims of his rampages, was the owner liability imposed by studs. Most horse liability issues favor the owner by implying that equine activities are inherently dangerous and basically, if you get hurt, it's your own damn fault. This changes somewhat with stallions and jack asses. When equines are left with testicles intact, they're known to be far more aggressive and dangerous, and owners are assigned significantly more liability.

While I'd never been overly concerned with safety and/ or liability issues, some of Joshua's antics were starting to get my attention, especially his "free range" breeding program during his periods of escape. While he didn't do too well breeding the mares I wanted him to breed, he seemed to have much better success out choosing his own mares. The only guest ranch mare to show up with a baby mule the next spring was one we'd rented from a long-time friend of Scott, the fancy dressing wrangler. The mare's owner, Nate, was also Scott's godfather and mentor, and he'd never much cared for me in the first place, strongly disapproving of Scott's association with a long-haired hippie sort of half-assed cowboy.

As unlikely as it is that anyone would rent a highly valued, prize mare to a dude horse operation, that seems to be exactly what Nate had done. Suddenly, this unnoteworthy old mare turned out to have some of the best bloodlines possible from champion cutting horses, capable of producing multi-zillion-dollar foals, which had been his plan, had Joshua not preempted the situation. I offered to buy the foal at a generous price and pay for the summer's lost rent on the mare, but that merely fed his fire. He threatened to sue me, beat me up, shoot Joshua (one of several such threats), and a few other aggressive actions. He was mostly trying to show off for Scott while also demonstrating what a worthless, irresponsible, chickenshit sort of drugstore cowboy I really was.

He actually stood up as fast as he could (he was as bent and busted up as any old cowboy), threw down his cane, saying he didn't want to be accused of using it as a weapon, and challenged me to get up and fight. I remained seated on a stump in front of him, trying to figure out what to do. He started shouting and cussing me out and asking why I wouldn't get up and fight like a man.

I knew that this was all bluff and bluster for Scott's benefit and that he didn't really want to fight any more than I did, but he was working himself into a frenzy and was starting to turn some frightening shades of crimson. At a total loss for what to do, I finally sputtered out that I would hate to beat up an old man even worse than I would hate being beat up by an old man, and I really couldn't figure out how to come out ahead in this situation so if he wanted to hit me, he might as well hit me while I was sitting. He huffed and chuffed around a little longer before storming off, telling me over his shoulder that I would get what was coming to me sooner or later.

That was probably the worst, but by no means the only, confrontation I had over Joshua, one of which almost landed me in jail. About a month after my confrontation with Nate, I got into trouble with a neighbor and the Boulder County sheriff. I was keeping Joshua with my mares, Lilly and Blossom, on some family property I was camping on close to Allenspark, Colorado. It was a pretty half-assed fencing situation for an escape artist like Joshua, but they had plenty of room and Joshua was so smitten with his new girlfriends that I was pretty sure he wouldn't be going anywhere. That proved to be true until a neighbor's mares came into heat.

Upon finding them missing one afternoon, I grabbed some halters and lead ropes, located where they'd ducked the fence, and started tracking them toward the neighbor's place that had the mares. Approaching their corrals, I heard the squelch of hand radios and slowed to a stealthier pace, staying out of sight. Soon I could see my critters in a coral where someone in uniform sat on the top rail. I was preparing to confront this person, who appeared to be an officer of some sort, when his radio sounded off again. While I was too far to hear what was said, the officer hopped off the fence and headed down the dirt road toward the highway.

I took advantage of his absence to run down to the corral, watching the road as I went. Through the trees, I could see a large gooseneck horse trailer with a Boulder County Animal Control insignia backing up toward the corral. The dirt road was crooked and difficult to maneuver (especially for a government employee sort), which is why the other officer had been called back to assist. This gave me plenty of time to halter my animals and take off riding Fart Blossom, the only one of the three manageable bareback with only a halter and lead rope, leading Lilly with Joshua following. Not knowing whether they might have riding animals or even try to track me on foot, I headed away from my pasture, proven worthless for securing them anyway, and toward forest service land where I could intersect a trail leading several miles to where a friend had a corral that couldn't be seen from the road.

A few days later, I was at my camp splitting firewood when a young lady in a Boulder County Animal Control uniform approached me.

"Are you Jim Duke?" she asked.

"Why? What do you want with him?" I replied.

She smiled. "OK. Listen and don't be a smartass. I know you're Jim Duke because we met at Lane Guest Ranch a couple years ago when some of his horses got loose. You seemed like a nice guy and you were good with the horses, so I'm only trying to do you a favor. You pissed off some people the other day and there's a warrant out for your arrest. I should arrest you right now and haul you in, so don't give me any more shit or I will. More importantly, the horse owner has sworn he'll shoot your jack if he ever shows up again, and he'd be within his rights to do so. Those are some very expensive Arabian broodmares he has. I think he's serious about this and I'd hate to see that cute little burro get shot. Anyway, you'll be receiving a warrant in the mail, but you should get to the courthouse and take care of this. They're looking for you and will arrest you if they find you."

Once again, I was amazed by how much mares seem to appreciate in value when they're exposed to jack asses. I thanked her for her concern and efforts on our behalf and assured her that Joshua was safe and secure. I'd been bouncing around between Allenspark, Ft. Collins, and occasionally Texas for the last few years and hadn't had a mailing address for quite a while, so I never received the warrant and promptly forgot about it.

About a year later, however, I got pulled over in Estes Park for a burned-out taillight, of all things. After running my record, the cop came back to my truck and asked if I was aware that I had a warrant out for my arrest—something about horses at large. "Sorry, Mr. Duke, but I'm going to have to take you in." Right then his lights flashed and his siren gave a short bleep. He ran back to his car, got on his radio, and returned to tell me he had an emergency and couldn't deal with me right now, but that I needed to take care of this immediately or I would be in jail soon.

A few days later, I went to the courthouse in Boulder to address the situation. After punching in my info, the lady across the counter looked at me and asked if I was aware there was a warrant out for my arrest. I told her that was why I was there. She told me to stay right where I was, that she would be right back, and rapidly disappeared through the door behind her. I followed suit and disappeared through the door behind me.

I then called the courthouse and arranged a hearing date. At the hearing, the judge read me the charges, which included "horses at large, knowingly and willfully grazing public lands, and evasion of law officers." He asked me how I pleaded. The first thing I said was that I didn't own horses (technically true; I only had one horse).

The judge stared ominously at me and then turned his gaze to the officer involved, who responded, "Well... um... Your Honor, I believe they might have been mules or donkeys." (Apparently, he'd forgotten there was a horse involved.)

The judge turned back to me. "Were you knowingly and willfully grazing public lands?"

"No, sir," I replied. "When I discovered they'd escaped, I tracked them directly to the corral where I recovered them. I don't believe they ever crossed public lands."

Again, the judge turned to the officer.

"Your Honor, that allegation came from the owners of the horses who told us that Mr. Duke was known for letting his animals free range on public lands," he responded.

The judge turned back to me. "Is this true, Mr. Duke?"

"No, sir. Other than my burro getting loose a couple times. I've never intentionally let them run free."

The judge gave a heavy sigh. "How about this charge of evasion?"

"I never saw anyone chasing me," I replied. "I just got my critters and took them home. I only had halters and lead ropes, so it's not like we took off at a run." (This was a bit of a stretch because we'd left at a pretty good clip. But there is a difference between a lope and a dead run.)

The judge turned once more to the officer.

"Well, Your Honor, we never really saw him... um... so we never really pursued him. We'd left the animals momentarily to back the horse trailer in. But he did it so quickly it had to be intentional."

Another heavy sigh. The judge didn't look up at me again but merely flipped the paperwork into a stack. "Case dismissed!"

By the time of that hearing, I'd already been out of the breeding jack business for almost a year. Having spirited my critters away from Boulder County authorities and having dealt with old Nate and any number of others Joshua had pissed off during that first year of running around causing trouble, it was getting to be a constant hassle. And that's not even counting the many affected folks I never had to deal with. I was hearing stories of baby mules mysteriously showing up from Estes Park to Nederland. Unfortunately, this was long before mules started enjoying their current popularity and most folks weren't too pleased with these little blessings, which is hard to understand for anyone who's ever seen a mule foal. There's nothing cuter on earth.

I would gladly have gone around and tried to purchase any and all of those unwanted foals, but I'd already learned how valuable all these mares became after the fact, and was sure I couldn't afford to start that process. Neither did I have any idea how much other damage Joshua had done along the way and didn't really want to get the word out on who might have been responsible. I took Joshua down to Ft. Collins that winter while I took a few classes at CSU, hoping his reputation in the Allenspark area might die down in the meantime. And while his reputation did calm down in that area, he earned a new notoriety around Ft. Collins.

College Cowboy

Meanwhile, during my years of trying to be a cowboy, dude ranch wrangler, and mule breeder, I'd managed to bullshit my way into college and worked a few random semesters at various schools into my schedule. Although I tested well on entrance exams, I'd never graduated from high school and had a poor GPA to boot. I was accepted at the University of Wyoming on a probationary code requiring that I maintain at least a 3.5 (B+) GPA pending the arrival of my high school diploma. The same probation requirements followed me to the University of Texas, where I took a few courses around ranch work. By the time I applied at CSU in Ft. Collins, with a 3.5 GPA from two other major universities, they quit asking for my high school diploma.

Being on probation those earlier years is probably the only thing that got me through college.

In much the same way that I never quite fit in as a Texas cowboy, I never really fit in as a typical college student either. Even though CSU was a hardcore Ag school, my lifestyle and collection of critters was a little extreme on campus:

Jackass Out of Control

As Stan pounded harder, the backstage doors of Sam's Old Town Ballroom finally flew open, the bright lights and blaring music of the Kamikazi Klones causing our mounts to spook and spin around to face the wall of police officers closing in on us.

It was the big spring festival at Colorado State University, then known as "College Daze." My friend, Stan, and I had decided to ride through town, he on his fat mare, and me on my little burro. Passing numerous "block parties" along the way, we'd been offered and had accepted every sort of party favor. By the time we got to the center of town, my brain was buzzing so wildly that I couldn't tell if all the noise and bright lights were outside my head or inside. Our goal was to ride into a bar.

The closest cop shouted, "Freeze, cowboy!" but Stan didn't even hesitate as he spurred his hippo-mare through their ranks. No sane person would have stood in her way. Joshua, my donkey, however, wasn't nearly as large and intimidating as the mare and was also much more cautious. He was as shocked and flashlight blinded as I was, and he froze as the cops closed in. The closest cop spread his arms in front of us and shouted, "Don't even think about it!!" Josh was actually shaking with fear and starting to realize that he'd been ditched by his beloved mare for whom he would have run through hell, which is exactly what he was preparing to do.

While all equines are gregarious and dislike being alone, this relationship went far beyond the norm. Joshua was still an intact male ass or jack ass, as they're referred to when they still have testicles, so he was inherently crazy about any mare. But this hippo wasn't just any mare. She had an anomaly that resulted in a red, swollen protuberance poking out of her most private, personal parts that looked more than anything like a sore thumb. It was apparently irritating enough that she constantly held her tail aloft to avoid contact with it, giving her the appearance of what is referred to as "flagging" when a mare is in heat. This impression was further emphasized by a reaction similar to that of a person with chapped lips constantly licking them, causing her to imitate the hottest stage of being in heat, referred to as "winking." The combination of the two drove Joshua insane with lust and he was inseparable from the mare.

With the danger closing in and the mare disappearing from sight, I knew he was about to explode, but I held my hands up in submission and then leaned forward as if preparing to swing my leg over and dismount, except that instead of swinging off, I intentionally caught my heel under his flank, his most ticklish spot, and ignited the explosion, holding on for dear life and shouting, "Jackass outta control!" My small burro wasn't as intimidating as the hippo horse so the police didn't so easily yield but instead, attempted to close in and stop us. Joshua scattered them like so many bowling pins, except for the big, Irish-looking cop with a red handlebar mustache who got ahold of my shirt and tried to pull me off. I left him holding a good-sized chunk of my shirt tail while mag lights and ticket books flew past my head. We were soon catching up with the lumbering hoofbeats of the obese mare.

While we'd made our initial getaway, the night was young and the chase was just beginning. Although the police had the advantage of fast cars, we had the advantage of sidewalks, back yards, and especially the block parties, crowding streets to the exclusion of vehicular traffic. The police would drop a couple guys off at one end of a block party while the patrol car sped around to the other side to intercept us. There were no cell phones in those days, but news traveled fast and block parties would be looking forward to our arrival. The crowds would part like the waters for Moses, handing us beers and joints as we galloped past, and then closing in on the police trying to chase us on foot.

The chase went on through alleys and backyards and, at one point, into a garage where we hid when they had us temporarily surrounded with all escape routes cut off as they searched for hoofprints in the gravel. Stan got clotheslined a couple times in the dark by literal clotheslines. I was low-profile and ducked the clotheslines, but donkeys are extremely difficult to stay on bareback, as I was, because they have no withers and are shaped such that the rider is on the highest, widest point around with nothing to hang onto. When a donkey drops its head down, the rider has the sensation of trying to balance on a beach ball on the edge of a cliff. To make matters worse, asses instinctively distrust anything man-made, and this was Joshua's first trip to town. Every white line, change of pavement, curb, and manhole cover caused a spook, sudden stop, or dodge. Manhole covers were the worst because I couldn't see them in the dark and he wouldn't slow down but just sidestep. They were like little round bull's-eyes that I hit pretty consistently with a dull, metallic thud. Fortunately, I always kept hold of the reins and Joshua considered me to be part of his "herd" in this scary situation and never tried to ditch me.

We managed to evade police throughout the evening, but rather than try to ride our critters back out of town where we would have been fenced in on the road shoulder and easily trapped without obstacles and escape routes, we tried to hide them in town in a back alley behind some dumpsters near my apartment. I slept on the seat of my truck close by to keep an eye on them while Stan got a ride home, where he could borrow a horse trailer from a neighbor in the morning to sneak the critters out of town.

I was awakened at first light by the squelch of police radios. A sneak peek over the dash revealed the same large, Irish-looking cop who'd first tried cornering us at the bar. I lay low, listening to conversations until I heard them discussing a trailer to impound the animals. He wasn't watching as I got out of the truck to confront the situation but when he did see me, he came raging toward me, barely able to contain his fury enough to start reading me my rights. He was so mad his waxed mustache was quivering and he had a twitch below his left eye as he spoke. Upon finishing reading my rights, he approached while pulling handcuffs off his belt.

"What are the charges?" I asked.

"Evasion!" he snapped. "And animal abuse!"

I countered with, "The way y'all came at us with bright lights and loud radios scared the daylights out of my donkey. After y'all started throwing stuff at us, I couldn't have stopped him for anything. As far as animal abuse, you put everyone, especially our critters, in danger. Why were you after us in the first place?"

Now he hesitated. College Daze was notorious for getting out of control and every year, there were more and more accusations of excessive force and even police brutality. There had been scores of witnesses last night, all students.

As he hesitated, I could see the wheels turning. "Well," he finally said, "I could see you were having trouble controlling your animal... but that other guy!" He thought some more. "Tell you what, you guys go ahead and take care of these animals and then come down to the station. Your friend is going to have to answer for his actions." With that, he went back to his car and drove off. Things didn't seem quite right. That was too easy. He hadn't even asked my name, much less ID. I smelled a trap.

Making sure I wasn't being watched, I went into my apartment close by and called Stan. He'd gotten the trailer and was ready to come to town. I told him to go to a mutual friend's house a few blocks away and call me when he got there. Meanwhile, I set up watch at a window from which I could see the alley where the animals were. Pretty quick, a cruiser passed through this rarely traveled alley. In the half hour before Stan called, they seemed to be cruising the alley about every ten minutes. I updated Stan with this info and told him to hang tight, I would call him the next time they cruised by, and we would both take off to meet in the alley a block south of my place. The plan went smoothly, and we were soon headed out toward Horsetooth Reservoir, where our pasture was.

I then went home, and shaved my very heavy beard, and quit wearing my hat for a while. This changed my appearance enough that even good friends didn't recognize me. Over the next few weeks, I noticed the presence of the Irish-looking policeman with the red mustache cruising the neighborhood, both in his car and on foot, as well as in uniform and in plain clothes.

This would likely be a good ending point for this story, but there's more to it, including a somewhat convoluted moral. The moral of the story started with my having dropped out of high school and eventually lying about that to get into college. My high ACT scores allowed me to start college during a summer school session, when high school grades weren't, in those days, so highly scrutinized. But I was put on probation pending the arrival of my high school diploma. A condition of probation was maintaining at least a 3.5 grade point average. My diploma obviously never arrived, so the GPA condition of probation remained. If not for that condition, I would have almost certainly continued my wayward ways that had resulted in my dropping out of high school in the first place and if I'd finished college at all, it certainly wouldn't have been with a GPA good enough for grad school.

Several weeks after my wild ass ride through College Daze, I had an interview to try to get into a master's program. My prospective major professor listened patiently to my lengthy proposal to utilize pheromones, CO_2 gradients, lights, and sound traps for the large-scale capture of insect pests to reduce the use of pesticides while also creating a resource of the insects' nutritional value. Upon the completion of my presentation, the professor leaned forward to lock eye contact and asked, "Are you the guy that outran the cops on a jackass?"

It was the moment of truth. He seemed pretty strait-laced and I'd heard he was a Mormon from Utah. While I feared the truth would disqualify me, I suspected he already knew the answer. Many people had seen us that day and there had been stories circulating campus. I fessed up. He chuckled a little and told me that my proposal was interesting, but very involved and unlikely to get funded through an Ag school with connections to agricultural chemical companies. Then he sat back and asked if I would like to go to Alaska. He had a pre-funded project studying mountain goat habitat and diets that could make a good master's program. He added that the fishing up there should be pretty good that time of year. Turns out he was a "jack Mormon" from a ranch family and a bit of a rowdy himself, and he was mostly looking for good company for the summer.

So, mine isn't the moral tale most good parents would share with their children to provide guidance. It isn't the honorable story of honest, hard work leading to success. The things that got me through college were having dropped out of high school and then lying about it. What got me into grad school was getting high on drugs and outrunning the police on a wild jackass.

What, then, is the moral of this story? Well, I guess that sometimes the best thing to do is to sit on your ass and get high.

***

As poor a student as I'd been consistently from preschool all the way on through whatever little high school I ever attended, I suddenly started getting very interested in all my coursework and doing well with little effort. My cowboyin' in Texas had put me a year or two behind most of my age group, so as an old man of twenty-one, I fancied myself somewhat more rounded and experienced than my peers. As one so far behind in my education, I was viewed by most of them as a lost cause or hard luck story of some sort. This view started changing as I began to rank highest in more science classes. I assumed that my newfound ease in learning was due to my more worldly background. Having lived in the real world for a few years, I felt that I had more of a framework upon which to attach incoming information. Things seemed more relevant and pertinent to real life. I often found immediate practical application for newfound knowledge.

Tan My Hide

In a microbiology class at Colorado State University, we studied a Middle Eastern technique used for tanning leather. It was described as an example of the selective digestive abilities of enzymes produced by various microbes that can make leather more supple and flexible without losing strength. Many such microbes are found in the feces of herbivores. It was further explained that the uric acid in urine was also a valuable tool in tanning, as was the lecithin found in brains and, whether coincidentally or a gift from nature, it seems that most herbivore brains contain just enough lecithin to soften their own hides. How cool! Herbivores have a built in, handy dandy tanning kit!

Having always been interested in tanning hides and having purchased a couple different tanning kits with poor success, producing brittle, weak leather, I was sure I'd found the ultimate solution. CSU had a meats lab and I'd heard that raw hides could be purchased there for five bucks a piece. I bee-lined over there immediately after class in my old Ford truck, hoping that nobody else in class had picked up on this obvious opportunity and outrun me to the meat lab for any hides on hand. I found a couple guys out by the loading docks behind the lab and inquired about cow hides. They reported that there were a couple Black Angus hides in the building but didn't think I would want them because they were so covered with manure and urine that their regular buyer didn't want them and they'd already been sitting there for several days and were getting pretty ripe.

I couldn't believe my luck!! Not only were these hides pre-treated, but they were probably already half tanned! Like a poker player who'd just been dealt a royal flush, I tried to contain my excitement and not tip my hand as to the treasure they were offering. I acted casual and replied that I might still want them if the price was right, to which they informed me that if I could stand to touch them, I could have them but warned that they would be heavy because they still had their heads attached. Could it get any better? I even got the brains. Pre-treated, half tanned hides and the brains to boot! I was getting a whole tanning kit and the hides for free! I continued trying to act casual as I followed them to the hides, hoping they hadn't taken microbiology and wouldn't be apt to have last minute revelations as to the value of this gift.

It required a strong stomach to drag the hides into the back of my truck.

It also took a strong stomach and tremendous physical strength to drag them up the stairs to the back deck of my apartment. I lived right on campus in a second-floor apartment above a bank on the corner of College and Laurel. There was an outside steel stairway up to the patio area leading to my apartment. The patio I used as a back yard consisted of the gravel rooftops of the bank and several other businesses along Laurel Street, including a photography shop, a T-shirt shop, a picture framing shop, and a little health food market down at the end.

I got the hides laid out and decided I couldn't control my gag reflex long enough to start digging the brains out. It was late winter and the hides would soon freeze, making it more tolerable to harvest the brains. The microbiology class had provided only the science and not the actual process. Would they tan spread out like that? Did I need to put them in a tub of water? How long and what temperature? I had some research to do. This was back in the late seventies, long before Google or anything like that. Any computer research was done by geeks with huge stacks of punched out computer cards at the air-conditioned computer building on campus. The rest of us went to the library and submitted a literature search, hand-written on an index card, and expected to wait for weeks for a response. No big deal; the freezing weather would buy me some time.

Meanwhile, one of my part time jobs was working for a livestock trucking company east of town called Cactus Hill Trucking. I helped work cattle and sheep through the stock pens as well as feeding and watering when they were short-handed. It was lambing season and while they avoided shipping pregnant ewes, lambs were occasionally born in a trailer with little chance of survival. I'd picked up a couple of these orphans and was bottle-feeding them in the kitchen of my apartment.

I hadn't heard back from my literature search yet and the weather was getting warm and rainy. It was also time for mid-term exams and work was busy, so the tanning project went on hold. But the hides began to "tan" again on their own and were getting pretty ripe, so I dragged them to the far end of my deck and laid them out over some big metal boxes located there, hoping to air them out a bit.

A couple days later while I was feeding the lambs, there was a knock on the door. I opened it to a guy in gray coveralls advertising some sort of duct cleaning service. He looked at the lambs and then at me before pointing across the deck and asking if I knew anything about the two dead cows out on the rooftops. Propped up like that with the heads still on, they did look like dead cows and, under the circumstances, it was hard to deny any connection to them, but I did inform him that they weren't dead cows per se, only cow hides. This didn't seem to be a significant distinction to him as he let me know that I'd draped them on the air intake of the health food market at the end of the rooftops. Apparently, the owners had been desperately searching their store for the problem before calling the serviceman, very distressed that something had died in the ventilator system.

He watched long enough to make sure that I dragged the hides away from the vent system before leaving. Having loaned my truck to a friend, I had no way of hauling them off, so I got a ladder and hauled them up to the next roof level above my apartment and as far as I could get from windows and vents.

It was the very next day that I heard another knock on the door. This time, it was a representative of the absentee apartment building owner who had apparently heard from the health food market and, upon seeing the lambs, cited a no pets clause in the lease and evicted me effective immediately. He didn't say anything about dead cows, although the odor was still strong. I didn't bother to argue that livestock weren't technically pets, nor that there must be some sort of grace period for eviction. I was starting to feel a little crowded in this neighborhood anyway, and I wasn't even listed on the lease in the first place.

I'd originally moved in, crashing on the floor of some friends who were caretaking for some other friends who had left for the summer and never returned. My friends had also eventually drifted off. I sometimes wondered if that had to do with my rowdy sheep trucker crowd who occasionally partied and crashed at the apartment. But nah, there are many reasons for folks drifting off, aren't there?

By that evening, I was crashing on the floor with my lambs at an unofficial "fraternity" of rowdy drinking buddies in their large, rented house, still on Laurel Street across from campus, and appropriately known as Animal House after the recent John Belushi film. I soon moved my camper trailer into their back yard, put up a fence, and moved in my horse, donkey, and two mules, where we all lived for another six months before being evicted again, this time by City Animal

Control. I would probably have lasted longer if my raccoon hadn't found her way into the restaurant two doors down during dinner hour. I finally realized that cowboys don't do well in tight quarters, and I moved a little ways out of town. I never did discover how the tanning turned out.

It seems noteworthy that one of the residents of the Animal House was the guy who had opened the back door of the bar that Stan and I had tried riding into prior to our College Daze race across town from the cops. While I hadn't gotten a look at him that night, he recognized me and was anxious to get acquainted. Like myself, he'd worked for a few years after high school before entering college and was a bit older than the crowd. He—Steve Jackson was his name—and I hit it off immediately in a life-long friendship. Steve, editor of the CSU student newspaper at that time, eventually became a successful and well-known author and owner of a publishing company. He's the one who has encouraged me to write this book and guided me in its completion, for whatever that's worth.

I often took college friends riding, many of whom had never ridden or been around large animals before. This was compounded by the fact that I had no idea how inexperienced I really was, resulting in all the horses and mules I'd proudly trained by myself turning out to not being very well trained after all, what is referred to as "green broke" at best. Inexperience fueled by over-confidence led to too many precarious situations that miraculously never caused any serious injury to riders or critters.

The Crossing

I don't remember the beginning or the end, only the middle of the story. I don't remember driving to the trailhead, where we parked, or anything about the trail. Only the crossing. I don't even remember how we got back across the river afterward or back to the truck, but I do remember every detail about crossing the river in the first place. It was one of the most ridiculous and naively dangerous things I've ever done.

My friend, Rich (another Animal House resident), and I had decided to go for a ride that day, the first nice day after some rainy spring weather. This was just another typical day for me, other than crossing the river, which I hadn't done before on my own mules. I'd swum horses before, mostly just in ponds, but asses are instinctively afraid of water in the first place, and mine hadn't ever been introduced to this experience before.

Asses are afraid of water for a number of reasons. Desert prey animals are most vulnerable at watering holes because, unlike regions with abundant water sources, predators can more easily stake out water holes. River crossings in Africa, where wild asses evolved, are also extremely dangerous due to alligators. The fact that asses can go days without water and then drink up to 40% of their body weight at one time further increases their vulnerability to predators. Cowboys experienced at roping wild horses will keep their own horse loping in tight circles, downwind and out of sight from a water hole, to keep their animal warmed up while the wild horses are cooling down and loading up with water, significantly slowing them down. Think of the difference made by a few extra pounds added to a horse in what is referred to as a "handicap race" and you can imagine the difference made by a couple hundred pounds of water.

Furthermore, the asses' small hooves that aid in their agility and sure-footedness can be a disadvantage in soft, boggy, or muddy situations, causing them to sink more easily. Floundering in boggy water holes is a leading cause of death among asses. Further exacerbating this situation is the fact the one of our riding animals, Joshua, was an intact male, with the added opinionated obstinance that comes with a set of testicles.

Fortunately, our other riding animal, Fart Blossom, was an exceptionally cooperative little mule, far more willing than most to forgive any abuse caused by my frequent poor judgment, and eager to please and do almost anything asked of her. These qualities are what enabled us, against the better judgment of both animals, to cross that icy cold, flood-swollen river. And Joshua, in addition to being very gregarious and "herd bound" as all equines naturally are, was uncommonly smitten with and attached to Blossom. He would have endured the fires of hell or, even worse for a donkey, a wild river, to stay with his love.

Being from Chicago, Rich probably hadn't ever ridden before, much less bareback in the mountains as we were doing. The combination of his enthusiasm and naive faith in my judgment, and my own cocky over-confidence, created the perfect storm of stupidity. When we got to the river, it seemed like an interesting challenge and good adventure, and it never really dawned on me, even after the fact, what sort of danger I was getting us into. Horses and (although reluctantly) asses, too, are strong swimmers, but even with large horses and in calm water, riders should lie flat to float along their backs instead of sitting upright and putting extra weight on them, especially when they're first learning to swim with a rider. We had all odds against us in this crossing.

We stripped down and left our clothes on the bank to keep them dry and, after many tries to coax them across while riding bareback with only halters and lead ropes (I rarely used bridles and bits in those days) and therefore without nearly as much control as provided with bridles and bits, we finally decided to lead them across while swimming ahead of them in the daunting spring runoff. Trying to stay ahead of a panicked mule in swift water is no easy feat, and speaking of feet, if they'd caught up and overtaken us, it's doubtful we would have ever surfaced again after being churned under by those striking hooves, kicking powerfully through the water. The resistance of the water would have held us in place while we got pummeled, instead of allowing us to roll with the punches, and thus would have magnified the power of each kick, like getting punched with your head against a wall—repeatedly.

And the same way a scared dog (or person) will try to claw its (their) way on top of anyone close by, mules are guided by this same tendency. Even when trying to lead an inexperienced mule across a shallow stream on foot, it will often take a wild leap and try to land exactly where you're standing, whether you're on foot or mounted. The mule will apparently figure that wherever anyone else is standing is the only place it knows for sure will provide solid footing.

At one point in crossing, Blossom, in a total panic, tried turning around to head back. Pulling hard as I swam, I pulled her over backward and she went completely under for a second, coming up blowing, snorting, and in an even worse panic. My poor, sweet little Blossom. She was the kindest, gentlest little angel I've ever known and didn't deserve the likes of me. While I never would have intentionally abused her, I was a pretty wild young cowboy sort in those days, always looking for adventure, and she was always caught in the middle of it.

We fortunately made it across without further incident, but as soon as Blossom struck solid ground, she went totally limp and started sinking backward into the current. I had to pull hard to keep her head above water and to keep her from washing away. I'd never seen anything like it and thought she'd had a heart attack and was dead. I felt awful and overwhelmed with guilt and was on the verge of tears when she exploded back to life, almost trampling me as she scrambled up the bank. I still don't know what really went on, but I guess she must have fainted.

Anyway, we still needed to retrieve our clothes from the far shore so I started looking for a place to tie the mules while we swam back. Rich, however, insisted that he was a very strong swimmer and that there was no reason for both of us to go back through that icy cold water on that chilly spring day. I hated being a wimp, but the chill in the air and the thought of the even colder water rendered me easy to convince of his logic, so I held the mules and watched him swim back for our clothes. The weather was still cool enough that we'd worn a lot of clothing, so when he had everything rolled up into a large spool around our shoes, he could hardly reach high enough to try to balance it on his head. It seemed obvious that this wasn't going to work, so I told him to wait for me to tie the critters up and come help, but he was determined and insistent and started back before I could get started across.

For the first halfway across, he was struggling but doing amazingly well with a one-armed breaststroke, barely catching an occasional breath between kicks. Then one loose pant leg flopped down over his face and, regardless futile head shaking and efforts to flip it out of the way, it started water logging and interfering with his breathing as it slowly dragged him down. I would have been quicker to his rescue had I not been helplessly rolling on the ground in laughter. Finally, his situation became desperate enough that he shifted his arms and made a one-handed pump shot with the wad of clothes toward the shore, but came up about ten feet short.

The sight of our clothing unraveling and rapidly spreading downstream with the current brought me to my senses and I dove in to start retrieving stuff as Rich struggled to shore, coughing and gagging. After several trips back and forth, grabbing the last of our socks as they disappeared, sinking into the murky spring runoff, I stood on the shore scanning for any remaining items bobbing or sinking through the current. Unbelievably, it seemed that I'd recovered everything. With wet matches for soggy weed, we had no way to make a fire. We were probably both approaching hypothermia by then and decided to dress in our wet clothes, hoping to get more warmth that way than by standing around naked, waiting for them to dry. That's when I realized my truck key was missing.

It was a single key without a key ring or fob or anything connected to it and was now located on a muddy bottom about six or eight feet deep in murky water, somewhere about ten feet offshore, somewhere in a twenty- to thirty-foot-long stretch along which our clothes had floated before I'd gathered them all.

Rich insisted that there was no possible way to find the key and that we would have to go break a window to get in and figure out how to hotwire the truck. We'd parked in a very remote spot with little chance of finding anyone around within about ten miles. I re-stripped and dove back in completely blind in the murky water, merely feeling along the bottom, squeezing the mud through numb fingers, hoping I could recognize the feel of a key if I encountered it. It was on my third dive and probably the last I was capable of, that I came up with the key.

I don't remember how we got back across the river. I don't remember the ride back to the truck or where we'd parked or driving home. All I remember is the middle of the story. The crossing.

***

I eventually gave up on the notion of Joshua as a breeding jack and had him castrated, hoping it might settle him down enough to be more useful as a riding animal. I started riding him around town for the first time since our police incident almost a year earlier with the intention of getting him accustomed to all the sights and sounds of the city. It was during one of these training sessions in downtown Ft. Collins that he got overwhelmed by traffic and sat down in the middle of a major downtown intersection.

One of the motorists stuck in the resulting traffic jam was a woman who got out to help urge Joshua across the intersection. She was patient, gentle, and helpful and asked if I would consider selling Joshua. By then, I'd learned that a gentler approach was required for mules and asses, but I'd already lost my temper and been too heavy-handed with him too many times. I knew I would probably never be able to earn his trust. He already seemed to trust and like her.

It turned out that her home and pasture were only about a mile out of town, so I followed her directions to the place and gave her Joshua for a promise to keep him forever—and for a ride home.

Gunther

The next spring on April Fools' Day, about a year after I'd had Joshua castrated, the mean little mare I'd bought to breed to him almost two years earlier gave birth to a surprise mule foal. With the mare being a very light-colored palomino, the foal was a beautiful, line-back buckskin, with seven black stripes around each leg, making him look very zebra-like. That beautiful little foal taught me how hereditary disposition is.

I'd always assumed that high-strung, spooky, or anti-social behavior among equines was the result of previous abuse. While this might be true with many bad habits, I'm now convinced that much of such behavior is hereditary. My ill-tempered little mare was, among other challenges, very head shy and extremely difficult to bridle. I was certain that someone had slapped her face too many times or, more likely, "eared her down," a common practice among bad animal handlers that involves grabbing an ear and twisting it while pulling down. It's an effective restraint, one I'd used myself before I knew better, but almost guaranteed to make an animal head shy. After a couple years of trying to gentle my mare down, I'd finally given up and started using a bridle without a browband or throatlatch so I could buckle it behind her ears without having to pull anything over them.

This sweet little mule foal, whom I named Gunther, was the culmination of years of dreams. I wanted us to be best friends and went to extremes to be as kind and gentle as possible. I groomed and petted him every opportunity and tried to work through any ticklish or touchy spots. While much better than his mother, he never really did learn to enjoy attention and buddy up with me. He not only turned out to be head shy, but his movements and idiosyncrasies were identical to his mother's. I've since noticed many such quirks, such as nervous head tossing and various ticklish spots on animals, that are identical to such quirks in their mothers.

But his lack of affection didn't set me back much. Like the girl who plays hard to get, it merely made me love him all the more and try that much harder. His high strung, nervous disposition made training challenging, but I was always looking for thrills back in those days and was soon riding bareback with only a bosal type bridle without a bit. A bosal consists of a rawhide loop that goes around the muzzle and creates enough leverage against the lower jaw to generally provide adequate control. They're commonly used in training young animals prior to using a regular bridle with a bit. With Gunther being as head shy as his mother, this was the easiest sort of headstall to get on. This allowed me to bridle him the same way I had to bridle his mother, by buckling it behind his ears like a halter rather than trying to go over his ears.

I rarely used bits back in those days anyway and could train most animals to be very manageable riding with only a halter. By then, I could ride Blossom with relatively good control with no headstall at all even at a dead run. I was also starting to work her in harness and could control her from the ground with only voice commands. But she was an incredible animal who loved to please and could practically (if not in reality) read minds. This was not the case with Gunther.

Among other things, Gunther tended to be a bad runaway. I tried a couple varieties of snaffle bits, the customary "starter" bits, but this, compounded by his head shy nature, only created more conflict with little, if any, added control. One of the best remedies for runaways, given enough time and space, is to let them run as far and fast as they want and then keep pushing them until they really want to stop. Every time they break away, you push them farther until they finally get tired of it and learn to stop when asked or end up having to run much farther than they want to.

About a dozen miles north of Fort Collins, an irrigation ditch paralleled by an access road ran for miles and miles without other roads, gates, or obstructions of any sort. The ditch was a very large one, dropping almost fifteen feet from the road and, being early fall, it was mostly empty with only a few puddles along the bottom. The other side of the road was delineated by a five-strand barbed wire fence. While it seemed at the time to be a fairly secure situation to keep him contained in one direction, I believe, in retrospect, that Gunther was athletic enough and crazy enough to have negotiated the boundaries on either side without breaking stride.

I started loping down the road and, as expected, he took off. I tried to rein him in a couple times and, finding only resistance, I started kicking and quirting, and the race was on. Mules are known for their stamina and endurance and after a mile or so, he was still going strong. Then we came around a bend in the road and about a hundred yards ahead I saw a great blue heron that had been hunting a deep pool in the ditch. The heron spooked and started to fly, but was struggling to gain altitude to top out of the deep ditch and had to fly level to stay ahead of us.

It was an exciting little race and Gunther seemed to enjoy it even more than I did. He dropped into an even faster gear and started to overtake the bird, putting us almost directly above it. Then, just as we were coming abreast of it, the bird regurgitated and jettisoned a several-pound carp, allowing it to rise up and bank hard out of the ditch. As the bird banked away from us, Gunther started turning as if to follow it and I thought we were going off the edge. But he managed to zig-zag straight again, almost putting us over the brink as he tight-roped along the edge of the ditch, sending down a cascade of rocks and dirt clods into the ditch. The bird, the ditch, and the near-death adrenaline rush have been forever emblazed on my brain.

I experienced too many near-death adrenaline rushes in Gunther's short life. In addition to being one of the most high-strung and spooky animals I've ever known, he was also extremely athletic and as agile as a gazelle. He was always wild and unpredictable and I loved him all the more for it. Everything about him, from his coloration and trim build to his wild attitude and quick, evasive moves, dodging unseen lions and other monsters, made me feel as though I was riding a large deer instead of a mule. I even started having dreams about riding a deer through dense forests at incredible speeds, dodging, leaping, and flying through the air over logs and gullies.

I often tried to emulate these dreams in real life, careening through aspen groves at breakneck speeds while barely, if even at all, in control, and where failure to act in unison with my mount could have resulted in serious injury or death. Having entered wild horse races at Cheyenne Frontier Days, having been a novice bush pilot suffering many close calls, and having been in general a thrill-seeker most of my life, I've never come close to the rush of those crazy rides through the timber.

I was devastated when Gunther died. And being at a point in my life where crying and general displays of emotion didn't seem to be an option, I had no tools to wash away my grief. Even in the midst of my sorrow, I was likely at least subconsciously aware that his death had probably saved my life, but that seemed unimportant. Nothing makes us feel more alive than almost dying, and I associated my most intense moments of living with that dangerous little mule.

I'd gone to spend Christmas with my brother's family for some back-country skiing just outside of Jackson Hole, Wyoming. One of the worst blizzards in years was blowing through the Rockies, and we were preparing for some of the best skiing ever. Then I received a phone message from a friend who was tending my critters in my absence. My small herd was on pasture about ten miles north of Ft. Collins with about a dozen other horses. The blizzard had drifted hardpack snow over fences throughout that region. This sort of hardpack snow, common to windy regions like Wyoming and the Dakotas, can be dense enough to drive a car over without sinking or, likewise, to support the hooves of animals, allowing them to walk over fences, as mine and many others from surrounding ranches had done. Running loose with scores of other equines, Gunther was apparently the only one to be struck by a vehicle.

Against all logic, since he was already dead and the rest of my animals had been confined, I felt compelled to leave immediately in the middle of the still raging blizzard to return home. Driving my little Volkswagen Rabbit way too fast in poor visibility, I nearly lost control trying to slow down to the speed of two State snowplows driving side by side, clearing the interstate. I regained control just in time to see the semi-truck jack-knifed in my rearview mirror a split second before he rear-ended me and shot me, as though out of a cannon, through the narrow slot between the two huge snowplows. Even after his life was over, Gunther had provided me with one last near-death experience to remind me of how alive I still was.

Lilly

Not much has been mentioned thus far about Gunther's mother, Lilly. She was, in fact, not very noteworthy other than being ill-tempered, extremely head shy, anti-social, and just plain dangerous. I'd always assumed that such behaviors were generally the result of past mishandling and abuse. And while this is often the case, it required the raising of two mule offspring of hers for me to realize how much of this sort of behavior is hereditary. With great reluctance, I've finally come to the conclusion that some equines are simply not worth dealing with. Most good and honest trainers will agree with this. While experienced trainers may choose to work with such animals for the purpose of some exceptionally desirable quality in that individual, beginners should never take on such animals with hopes of changing their behavior.

The category of ill-tempered equines doesn't include frightened animals. Any wild (feral) or range-raised horse will likely be terrified by any initial confinement by and contact with humans. While such animals can still be extremely dangerous and aren't recommended for handling by beginners, they can rapidly learn to trust humans and become safe and reliable companions. But there are some that will remain unpredictable (or predictably mean) all their lives and can never be trusted. While I didn't know her history that might have caused her behavior, and I wasn't a good enough trainer to say absolutely that she couldn't have been brought around, I suspect that she never could have been totally trustworthy.

I got her to the point that, other than being head shy and spooky, she at least tolerated, and maybe even liked me a little, and I felt reasonably safe around her. I could never, however, trust her around others, especially when she had a foal at her side to defend. After many close calls with snapping jaws, strikes, and kicks, she finally actually kicked someone (not too seriously) and I had to get rid of her. I found her a good home with a working cowboy packing salt in remote ranges, where she wouldn't have contact with too many people.

Even though I'd never been as fond of Lilly as I had been of Gunther, and it wasn't as if she died, I felt bad about having to give her up, even though doing so probably saved me from serious injury. But I feared for her future if she didn't settle down, and I missed the weirdly addictive near-death thrills she provided a little too often, as when I tried to harness break her.

Jumping Jehoshaphats

"Good judgment is the result of experience and experience the result of poor judgment." - Mark Twain

"Jumping gee horse fat?" I'd never known the exact phrase nor its origin and doubt that anyone has ever given it much thought. But it was explained to me in sort of an interactive revelation complete with a step-by-step demonstration.

There had been an early snowfall at my cabin near Allenspark, Colorado. I'd bid on a Forest Service timber harvest contract on about twenty acres east of town. This was back when ponderosa pine beetles were first starting to spread at alarming rates. The Forest Service had arranged to subsidize forest thinning to deter these infestations.

While most timber went to the highest bidder, as usual, the subsidies came into effect on the less accessible areas, allowing contractors to submit negative bids and get paid for the removal of timber. Some contracts paid as much as a hundred bucks an acre. I was fortunate enough to receive one of the worst contract areas in the county, most likely, in retrospect, because nobody else bid on it. I wasn't bothered by inaccessibility because I planned to skid logs out by draft animal. I was also undaunted by the fact that neither my mare, Lilly, nor I had any experience with driving in harness. This seemed the merest of details to such a capable team as my mare and me.

I had no doubt about her abilities. I'd never seen another horse run backward so fast while kicking in both directions every other step like she'd done when I tried catching her the first time. The closest I'd ever seen to moves like hers was a scene from an old Japanese war movie, where one warrior and his attack horse, striking, kicking, and biting in every direction, made short work of a whole village of angry peasants. She would have been the envy of any Cossack, Samurai, or other mounted soldier who didn't want to be bothered by primitively armed pedestrians.

My qualifications included some cowboying and dude ranching and a few rodeo events, such as having won the Bicentennial Boulder County Fair wild cow milking competition, but mostly consisted of my firm belief that I could do anything that anyone else could do, and a lot that others couldn't do. This affliction, which has plagued me my entire life and nearly ended it several times, has also occasionally worked in my favor. It can be described as an active lack of awareness that I call "applied ignorance." In a functional sense, it's not all that different from the noble quality known as confidence, merely a little riskier at times.

I'd been collecting all sorts of harness but was truly surprised by the complexity of it all. It's hard to tell where one set of harness leaves off and another starts. It took me quite a while to feel comfortable that I had a complete harness, not missing anything critical, and without too many extra parts hanging off it. I was also wishing I had a somewhat less ticklish mare to be sizing this all out on. Nonetheless, it wasn't too long before I had her all decked out and looking sort of like she was ready to go to work—except for the blinder bridle.

Most of the old harness I'd salvaged was sized for large draft horses. Although I'd been able to scrounge up a small enough collar and punch holes in the rest of harness to make it fit my small mare, it looked like it might take major surgery to get the blinders to fit properly. Anxious to get started, I convinced myself the blinders weren't all that important. I figured the blinders were mainly just to keep an animal from getting distracted, which didn't seem too likely considering her intense preoccupation with this whole deal. Maybe she wouldn't be so spooky if she could see what was going on behind her.

After first leading and then driving her around a little, practicing voice commands, she wasn't settling down too well, so I thought pulling a little weight might tire her out enough to calm her down some. I picked out a fairly good-sized aspen log that appeared heavy enough to slow her down and attached it to her single tree with about twenty feet of nylon climbing rope, thinking the log might not be as spooky at a little distance and the stretchy nylon might ease the jarring of her jerky movements.

Upon leaning into her harness and breaking that log loose from its resting place, Lilly immediately tried spinning around to see what had caused this strange phenomenon. I managed to get her straightened out and standing still, although shaking and snorting, and eased her into another step. She moved. It moved. She froze. She looked back at me, her eyes begging to be rid of the evil log. Then she exploded. I managed to hang on across the meadow, skiing, skidding, and stumbling along behind her and trying to stay out of the path of the log that was springing along behind like it was on a giant rubber band.

Entering the timber on the far side of the meadow, I was unable to maintain the reins through the trees without putting myself directly in front of the log, which by now had me as scared as it did her. Turning her loose, I watched helplessly as my mare disappeared down through the trees at breakneck speed. Although I couldn't see her, I could follow her progress crashing through the woods down below by the powdery white explosions that followed her as the log bounced between the trunks of the snow-laden trees.

Standing there on the hill, holding my breath against the impending silence that might signal a serious injury of my faithful friend, I saw the miniature blizzard start to circle back around in my direction. My heavy heart first lightened with hope upon the approaching clank and jangle of the harness, and then rocketed with adrenaline as Lilly crashed out of the woods, descending on me in her frantic quest for help. I sidestepped her initial assault, glancing off her shoulder and spinning around just in time to hop the nylon rope that was trying to wrap itself around my legs as she entered a tight circling pattern around me. For a few eternally long seconds, I played a life and death game of jump rope, geeing, hawing, and whoaing as calmly as a person can possibly scream. I became hopeful as she began to tangle in the traces, but as she tried to kick free, the rope swung high, sweeping my feet out from under me. I managed to donkey hop the rope on all fours and gain my feet again, but she'd kicked free of the coils and was going strong. I decided to follow her initial reaction and run for it. Pushing off her flank as she circled uphill, I made one last jump over the rope and started a post-holing sprint downhill through the deep snow. Like one of those slow-motion nightmares that won't allow full speed when so desperately needed, the sound of clanking harness and muffled hoofbeats started closing in behind me.

I'd almost made it to a big boulder at the bottom of the draw, where I hoped to scramble to safety, when I hit the deeper snow that had drifted in on its leeward side. The waist-deep resistance threw my upper body forward so that I face-planted just short of the boulder, where I assumed the fetal position and waited to be trounced.

It was so peaceful and quiet curled up there under the snow that I wondered if I'd passed painlessly into the hereafter. When I finally did venture a look, I saw my faithful mare a couple feet to my right plowed into the drift in much the same position I was in and venturing much the same look around. The echoes of the harness jangling and my own hollering were still going through my mind. Then it struck me—I'd been jumping, and geeing, and hawing so fast: JUMPANDGEEHAWSOFAST!

While I realized this was sort of a strange revelation in that situation, it was as welcome as the snow packed down my back, my rasping struggle for air, the crystal blue sky above, and all things having to do with life.

I would wager that back in the days when horses were more commonly used by a wide variety of people, such wrecks and precarious predicaments were common enough for this saying to have evolved. If anyone has the knowledge to prove me wrong, I guess I would just as soon not hear about it. Another one of the advantages of "applied ignorance" is the incredible freedom of thought it provides.

Everything that Kills Me Makes Me Feel Alive

No matter how you look at this lyric from OneRepublic's popular song "Counting Stars," it rings true and speaks volumes. Whether you consider all the unhealthy little bad habits we pick up along the way and then battle for the rest of our lives, or the big near-death experiences that are life-changing, this little phrase provides an apt description. Be it a strong coffee and a Camel straight cigarette or a beer and bong breakfast on a desert camping trip, these highs are hard to beat! I both envy and pity those who have never shared such experiences. Why do you think all the stuff that is so bad for us is so addictive? And many of these things that make us feel better literally do kill us. Probably the only moderation that allowed me to survive the addictive ways of my drug-ridden youth was the simple practice of "never pay for it, never turn it down."

When we get into the adrenaline rushes of near-death experiences, this phrase takes on a whole new and even stronger significance. Nothing makes us feel more alive than almost dying. Along these same lines, few things feel better than relief from discomfort. An old cowpoke once told me that he always bought his boots too small because taking them off at night was the only relief he ever got and he wanted to get the most from it. While most folks don't go out of their way to suffer, there's a lot of truth to this notion. Who remembers any details about the pleasant, uneventful camping trip where the weather was perfect and everything went according to plans? We all remember forever the times that a bear tore up the whole camp, or the storm that slammed the boat up against the rocks and threatened to drown everyone, or even the simple discomfort of limping back to the trailhead with cold, wet, sore feet and inadequate clothing in the driving sleet. These are the experiences we remember and come to cherish.

About fifty years ago, as a young wrangler for a guest ranch, I quickly learned that the closer our trail ride came to total disaster, but without any serious consequences, the livelier was the chatter around the bar at the lodge that evening and the better the tips. The wild lightning storms above timberline, encounters with hornets causing horses to take off bucking and running through the woods, or even the mere discomfort of the saddle and unfavorable weather bringing people to the point of tears by the time we get back to the lodge; we all want to be part of a good story. People hate and love being forced out of their comfort zones. Life is, after all, mostly a collection of recollections, a book of stories that should be anything but boring.

Everything that kills us makes us feel alive. This also seems to be particularly true of survivors of cancer, heart attacks, or other life-threatening conditions. Survivors of such life-threatening conditions generally seem to experience something along the lines of a new lease on life. Such people seem to come away with a whole new appreciation of life. Their priorities change to focus on the truly important aspects of living while avoiding all the petty little hassles that can consume so much time and energy. It's like the other lyric from one of Tim McGraw's songs: "Live like you were dying."

The concept of "significant emotional events" might explain much of this phenomenon. Hitler was probably the best known for promoting the notion of "give me a boy until the age of six and I will own him for life." This is probably true for the most part in the sense that our personalities in general are largely established at a relatively young age, after which time any major changes in character are brought about only by significant emotional events. These constitute events associated with so much fear, pain, trauma, and/or revelation that they cause permanent changes in our personalities, including the ways we feel, act, and view things.

Throughout history, people have endeavored to make life safer, easier, and more secure. Those who wrestled wooly mammoths for a living probably didn't need to pursue any additional adventure and excitement. Significant emotional, life-changing events probably occurred on a very regular basis. We have since succeeded in making life sufficiently safe and secure, for at least some of us, that there is now a trend toward seeking out danger and adventure. People are becoming more active in pursuing life-changing experiences. Such pursuits come in many different forms, from outward-bound types of intense outdoor experiences, to dangerously extreme activities, to drug-induced spiritual states such as ayahuasca ceremonies.

Most folks agree that change and personal growth are important to healthy lifestyles. If significant emotional events are indeed a primary force of change in our lives, this would indicate that very active, high-risk, and maybe even a little self-abusive lifestyles would be the healthiest lifestyles. It's as though one must be willing to risk life in order to fully live it. We must lose our fear of death to fully enjoy our lives.

While totally illogical, it is so true: everything that kills me makes me feel alive. It seems like those who are the most afraid of dying generally have the least to live for. Such people tend to be so concerned about their well-being that they're unable to enjoy many of life's adventures. They're so busy protecting their lives that they fail to live them. And realizing that they haven't really lived yet only serves to increase their fear of death—nobody wants to die without really having lived. For such folks, it might be a good time to go hunt a wooly mammoth with sticks and rocks. Maybe tease a saber-toothed tiger along the way. Or at least go on a white water raft trip or other activity that offers good thrills with minimum risks. But it must involve at least some risk. Otherwise, you're only going through the motions without really living it.

Since this chapter seems to be driven by lyrics, who better to close with than Garth Brooks? "Life is not tried, it is merely survived if you're standing outside the fire."

Duley

Lilly's second mule foal, Duley, from a different jack since Joshua had been castrated, was also chronically head shy and somewhat antisocial, but not nearly as crazy as Gunther had been. He was more of what equestrians refer to as a "rogue," in that he didn't like affection or attention. He was also a line-back dun with striped legs, but shorter, stockier, and not as sleek and beautiful as Gunther had been. He was quite a character with lots of personality who loved to follow me around, barely out of arm's reach, just to remind me that he didn't want to be petted. But as is common with mules, he loved to work and exert himself. The only times he would become affectionate were after he'd been worked to a lather. Then he would become my best friend and want to rub his sweat off on me and be brushed all over, including a little ear scratching, and would practically say, "Man! We did that together! Good work, pardner!" He became a heavy hauler and trusted friend of about thirty years.

But even after decades of friendship, Duley still maintained the basically antisocial and head-shy quirks he'd inherited from Lilly. He seemed to like me and always wanted to come along whenever he saw the horse trailer but could almost never show any sort of affection. He would only stand still for haltering if I shouted sternly at him, but he would scream like a baby if I ever threatened to leave him behind.

Blossom's First Job

With the passing of the Mined Land Reclamation Act in the mid-seventies, funding became available for the reclamation of historically abandoned mine sites. A college friend who had started his own reclamation business won a huge revegetation contract on a previously abandoned strip mine. The strip mine had become a favorite dirt bike/four-wheeler area, and part of the contract included closure from any motorized traffic. Upon completion of revegetation, there would be no more motorized equipment allowed on site, and all remaining work had to be completed by hand or draft animal to prevent leaving tracks that might attract other traffic. Knowing that I'd skidded wood with draft animals in the past, my friend offered me a very lucrative sub-contract to conduct the fencing with my mules.

I'd long since sold Lilly, the only animal I'd trained to harness, but I was confident that Blossom could easily take up the harness. She'd been by far the easiest animal I'd ever trained to ride. I'd basically just hopped on bareback with a halter and lead rope and, without ever offering to buck or spook, she'd picked up reining almost instantly. I'd also taught her voice commands, anticipating that I might someday use her in harness. As expected, she picked it up quickly and was ready for work in no time.

With the help of a friend who was handy at welding, I built a solid steel work buggy using four-foot-tall wheels from an old dump rake and designed the buggy for hauling fence posts and other materials, with attachments for a steel bar across the back to string out four spools of barbed wire at once. Blossom and the work buggy were very successful and things were going smoothly, including the revegetation efforts with strong germination and rapid plant establishment. Such was the success that the Bureau of Reclamation decided to showcase it with a huge volunteer workday and much publicity on Earth Day that year. They were particularly excited about showing off Blossom and her work cart and insisted that we be part of the celebration.

As we approached the center of activity on the big day, the little dirt road leading to the site became more and more crowded with expensive vehicles from the wealthy enviro-yuppie crowd attending the event. Mules are extremely suspicious of sudden and extreme changes in their surroundings and I could tell that all the commotion on this normally lonely site had Blossom on edge. I would have bailed on the situation and headed away from the celebration, but the cars were parked way too tightly for me to turn around or get off the road. Then a crowd of people descended upon us with loud chatter and cameras flashing. The polaroid type of cameras so popular in those days didn't merely flash but also produced every kind of beeping, buzzing, and dinging noise imaginable. As a guest ranch wrangler, I'd seen more than one dude cowboy clinging to a noisy camera as they flew through the air before our otherwise spook-proof horses became accustomed to this new technology.

Surrounded by expensive cars as the noisy crowd closed in, I started having visions of the old *Ben Hur* movie where the chariots were designed with cutting blade hubs to destroy the competition. The flimsy siding of these Audis and Porsches would be no match for the six-inch steel hubs of my dump rake wheels, while women and children scrambled over hoods and trunks of cars trying to escape the onslaught. Right when I thought things couldn't get any crazier, a news network helicopter zoomed in close enough overhead to kick up dust and debris. I braced for the worst, assuming that my lucrative employment and even my carefree life as I knew it were about to end in a bloody massacre.

Blossom merely planted her feet and froze! Finally feeling secure enough, I climbed out of the buggy and worked my way up the reins to her head to comfort and console her—or was it the other way around? At any rate, I knew right then that I would be forever indebted to that little mule and that I could trust her with anything, including my own children. I had as a partner what is referred to as a "bomb-proof" mule. In the next thirty or so years of our relationship, she never let me down.

Readers might have noticed that I refer to Blossom as a mule. Technically, if she was a mule, she should be referred to as a molly. But as previously mentioned, I don't think Blossom was a mule; rather, I believe she was a hinny. With all this confusion, it might be a good time to introduce some equine terminology.

Equine Nomenclature

Those who don't know the difference between a burro and a burrow don't know their ass from a hole in the ground.

Folks often ask me about the difference between donkeys and mules. I've become somewhat of an expert on this topic, keeping in mind that my main qualification as an expert has less to do with my own extensive knowledge than it has to do with everyone else's lack of knowledge. My level of expertise is further bolstered by the fact that the etymology of cowboy colloquialisms is hardly an exact science, providing lots of room for discretion (i.e. bullshit). Most references come word of mouth from old timers who are mostly dead and unable to repudiate. It's with these qualifications, along with the fact that nobody else really cares about this topic, that I offer the best dissertation on equine nomenclature that you're ever apt to receive.

There are horses, *Equus caballus*, and asses, *Equus asinus*, two different species in the same genus. They're closely enough related to be able to hybridize and produce offspring: the mule or hinny, depending on the sex of the parents. Mules are the result of a jack (intact male) ass bred to a mare. Mules are known as mollies (female) and johns (castrated male), although to old timers, the term "mule" implied a castrated male. There is no term for uncastrated mules because there's no reason to keep testicles on a sterile hybrid only to elevate testosterone to levels that cause males of all species to act like jackasses. Mules tend to be heavier boned and stronger than hinnies and are considered the superior of the two hybrids for draft work. They're often cited in genetics textbooks as a prime example of heterosis, or hybrid vigor, resulting from genetic diversity. Unlike mares, mollies are generally preferred for work and riding.

When a stallion is bred to a jenny (technically "jennet" but always "jenny" to cowboys) ass, the resulting offspring is known as a hinny, a name derived from the higher pitched combination bray (ass vocalization)/whinny (horse vocalization) compared to the generally more guttural call of the mule. Although genetically identical to their reciprocal cross, hinnies differ due to the maternal effects of the mare's womb compared to that of the jenny. Born of the jenny, they're generally smaller than mules but otherwise tend to be more horse-like in their features, although more variable in all characteristics and difficult to absolutely distinguish from mules without knowing their ancestry. Male and female hinnies are known as buds and blossoms respectively.

OK, I admit, I just flat-assed made up those last two names. But this seems justified to fill a void. There is so little said of these rarely encountered hybrids that I doubt there have ever been widely established names for the sexes. In the unlikely event that anyone ever refers to a hinny by sex, they will generally fall back on ass terminology, referring to them as jacks and jennies, unjustly diminishing the importance of hinny sexual identity. Considering the growing emphasis on gender distinction, imagine being born a sterile, half-assed, reciprocal hybrid without even clear species identification, and you might begin to understand the importance I place on hinny gender identity. For this reason, for the sake of completion of equine nomenclature, and to close an obvious and glaring gap in defined reality, I take the liberty of assigning hinny gender identity. Having spent more than half my life with a female hinny named

Fart Blossom, I dedicate that name to the female hinny and the logical counterpart, bud, to the male.

Going back to horses, males are stallions and females are mares. Babies are called foals, and male foals are colts while female foals are fillies. Breeding stallions are known as studs, breeding mares as brood mares. Castrated stallions are called geldings. Here again, to an old timer, the term "horse" implied gelding, as few rode mares back then. Mares were considered too moody due to cycling.

Back to asses, there are jacks, the males, and jennies, the females. "Burro" is the Spanish word for asses and mostly applied to the smaller, Mexican/Central American variety. The term "donkey," according to old timers, referred to a castrated jack.

It's noteworthy that in the Mexican culture, probably because equines are still commonly used in rural areas, equines are always referred to by sex. There are no generic terms for horses, mules, or burros that group the sexes together. *Caballo* refers to geldings, *yegua* refers to mares, and *semental* refers to stallions. A male mule is a macho and a female is a mula. Burro is male and burra is female. Hinnies are referred to as buds and blossoms (we need to establish this internationally).

Like other hybrids, mules and hinnies are generally sterile, although there have been many documented exceptions. One well documented case was a molly that gave birth to several foals, both mule and horse foals, recorded and studied at Texas A+M in the late 1950s. The only resulting conclusion was that "them aggies didn't know a jack ass when they had one" (i.e. see ass from hole in ground). Another well-known case was a molly that gave birth to a mule named Blue Moon in 1984. Blue Moon was exhibited at the Western National Stock Show for several years. There have been about fifty cases of fertile mules and hinnies over the past couple hundred years.

Some of the many advantages attributed to mules include increased strength and endurance, disease resistance, and feed efficiency. They also have better survival instincts and are far less likely to do something to endanger themselves, like spooking off a cliff, and are therefore safer in many situations. Some of these traits result from hybrid vigor, but some likely come directly from the ass half. Asses are not only smarter, but they haven't been nearly as screwed up through selective breeding as horses have. Modern day asses look very much like their wild type ancestors still roaming Africa. Selection for calm disposition and submission has bred survival instincts out of horses to help them accept training that often goes against instinct.

The reason asses and mules are reputed to be stubborn is because they aren't so willing to compromise their own survival instincts. They aren't so much obstinate as opinionated. Contrary to popular belief, asses are very predictable. They will always behave like asses, which includes being cautious and careful, often resulting in thoughtful hesitation. Pushy, demanding folks will find this behavior to be intolerable. Patient, understanding types might find this same behavior to be invaluable, especially if you want to ride with relative safety through dangerous areas like the Grand Canyon.

I live in an area abundant with burros and burrows without ever a problem in distinguishing the two. I have, however, occasionally been deserted in remote camps and unable to find my own ass with both hands.

Maybell

As word got out in the Range Science Department that I had mules and spent a lot of time in the back country, I started being offered work opportunities for my animals. I was offered a research associate position studying antelope winter habitat west of Maybell, Colorado. This position was offered largely because of my mules and my abilities in the back country from years of trail guiding. Antelope can cover long distances foraging in the winter, and it was decided that traveling by mule would be the best and safest way to keep track of herds in that rugged country. As it turned out, there was a record cold and snowy winter with drifts far too deep for any horse or mule, and I wound up tracking antelope mostly on my cross-country skis.

Living many miles from the nearest phone or electricity in one of those little, round-roofed sheepherder's wagons, the kind designed to be pulled by horses but more often now moved around by pickup trucks, I witnessed the coldest temperature ever recorded in the lower forty-eight states. There was a weather recording station in Maybell that year, and it reached -63° Fahrenheit without the wind chill factor. About twenty miles from pavement and regular snow plowing routes, I was often marooned for days or even weeks when the roads drifted in deeper than the best of four wheelers can handle.

One time, after over a week of -20° F. temperatures, it warmed up to almost zero and it felt like a reprieve. Having been too cold for my truck to start, even if the roads had been plowed, I hadn't been more than a few hundred yards from my sheepherder's trailer for ten days and decided to go for a ride. I rode bareback for the body heat and, without realizing there was any breeze, happened to take off down-wind in an unnoticeable 2-3 mph wind. Within a mile or two, I began to realize what a bad idea this was and turned around to return home. As soon as we began walking into the mild breeze, effectively doubling the wind speed to 6 mph, the effect felt like instant frostbite. My exposed face immediately started burning with the cold, causing me to have to dismount and eventually walk backward all the way home, leading my mule along.

As the winter worsened, I witnessed one of the worst antelope starve-offs ever. It was a long, cold, lonely winter with my only occasional neighbor being one of the Peruvian sheepherders who didn't speak any English but was otherwise very good company when we crossed paths. The ranchers in that region all hired South American sheepherders on two- or three-year contracts because the local, generally Mexican, sheepherders tended to disappear after a few weeks of sub-zero weather. The Peruvians had no connections in the country and nowhere to go. Many ranchers fed sheep and cattle with draft teams rather than tractors. This is not only because of the difficulty in starting tractors in sub-zero temps, but also because desperate sheepherders have been known to drive tractors to the closest highway and then hitch-hike south.

That winter reminded me, once again, what a social creature I was, not cut out for such long periods of intense loneliness. While that study could have continued for years with potential for a PhD dissertation, a temporary summer position in Aspen, Colorado reminded me how much fun a social life can be. While I was reluctant to give up on the antelope study, the harsh winter had killed off enough antelope that future funding might have been in jeopardy, and I was becoming disillusioned by the politics involved. The study had largely been funded by the Sheep and Wool Growers Association with the (unspoken) goal of showing that there were too many antelope, not too many sheep, degrading local habitat. With the huge die-off of antelope, it was likely that funding priorities might change.

While I loved wildlife studies, it seemed that the wrong team always had all the money. Even the mountain goat study for my master's degree, funded jointly by the Chugach National Forest and the Alaska Department of Fish and Game, was funded more out of financial concerns than for the well-being of the wildlife. Although not as extreme as the sheep vs. antelope herd study, the unspoken goal of the mountain goat study was to find anything, other than hunting pressure, that might be limiting the mountain goat populations. Their main goal was to maximize revenues generated through hunting.

Aspen

Aspen was like nothing I'd ever seen before, a beautiful region teaming with wealthy environmentalists. A place where the right team had all the money! Or so it seemed at first. It took me a few years to figure out how little difference there can be between environmental green and cash green. But in the meanwhile, I was able to bask in the popularity of a variety of environmental efforts with nearly unlimited support and funding. Through my position with Pitkin County, I started a revegetation program and recycling and compost operations. I was being paid more than ever before to merely pursue my own personal causes while living in a paradise of wilderness, hunting, fishing, skiing, biking, and everything I could possibly dream of.

In much the same way that racing the cops through the streets of Ft. Collins had opened the door to graduate school for me, my mules had, in a round-about way, created the opportunity for my dream life in Aspen. While I was still living in Ft. Collins, I'd started working summers for the Larimer County Agronomy Department, doing invasive weed mapping and control. I began pursuing non-chemical weed control efforts, including the grazing of goats on some weed species such as leafy spurge, and the use of insect weed eaters. My involvement with the insects led to another paid position for my mules and, eventually, paved the way for my job with Pitkin County.

My interest in insects for controlling weeds started with Painted Lady butterfly caterpillars. I'd noticed dense patches of Canada thistle eaten down to the nub by these caterpillars. It seemed that this should provide good weed control except that Painted Ladies are a very migratory species and, after eating down the thistle, the caterpillars pupate, become butterflies, and fly off before laying more eggs, giving the thistle plenty of opportunity to re-grow.

My plan was to raise these butterflies in captivity so that I could release fresh batches of caterpillars throughout the season, thus preventing any regrowth and depleting root reserves so the thistle couldn't survive. I also planned to do some selective breeding to weaken the migratory tendencies from my experimental population. The rapid results of selective breeding in insects have been demonstrated through a number of studies.

My selective breeding program would have been very simple. Since the spring migration of these butterflies is to the north, I would periodically open north-facing windows in my greenhouse long enough for 80-90% of the butterflies to leave. Those more reluctant to leave would remain as future breeding stock. It probably would have required only a few generations to produce a largely non-migratory population of Painted Lady butterflies. Part of the simple beauty of this effort would have been that these butterflies were already native to this continent, and I wouldn't have been introducing a foreign species with the potential of becoming a worse problem than the weeds they were supposed to control. Furthermore, because Painted Ladies do not over-winter at our latitudes, a non-migrating population of this species wouldn't survive in the wild and would be less likely to contaminate wild-type populations.

Fortunately, my breeding program never got off the ground. Such amateur efforts to tinker with nature never end well. Even many of the best thought out efforts by our top scientists often go awry, causing untold damage from the best of intentions. I could potentially have diluted migratory tendencies for the entire species, putting them at risk.

While my Painted Lady efforts never amounted to much, my interest in weed-eating insects and my position with Larimer County provided me with the opportunity to start working with the State Insectary in Palisade, Colorado. The insectary specialized in the use of introduced insect species for the control of weeds and insect pests.

When the insectary learned that I had mules and spent a lot of time in the back country, they arranged to hire me, through Larimer County, to ride the most remote parts of Larimer County and Rocky Mountain National Park to locate patches of musk thistle to release an introduced species of weevil that eats musk thistle seeds.

The only problem was that this weevil was, as any good biological control vector should be, so good at distributing itself where needed, that every patch of musk thistle I found, no matter how remote, already had a strong population of these weevils thriving. At first, I didn't tell anyone, rationalizing that sooner or later, I would start finding unpopulated thistle patches that would justify my efforts (and their expenses). But I finally gave in to guilt and told my county supervisor and the insectary about the widespread distribution of these weevils. Surprisingly, they weren't too interested in this discovery.

I'd assumed that I was forfeiting the best job I'd ever had. It seemed that the widespread self-distribution of a recently introduced weed-eating insect would be a success story to tout, but they were getting so much good publicity with such an attractive, environmentally sound (not to mention a little western) alternative to the widely unpopular herbicide applications that they wanted to continue the program. I kept my mouth shut, started carrying my fishing rod to work, and continued riding the high country and streams of Larimer County.

As previously mentioned, all these buggy pursuits on my resumé eventually provided me the sort of credentials beneficial to gaining employment in the tree hugging community of Aspen, Colorado. During my job interview, the otherwise disinterested environmental coordinator for Pitkin County perked up and took notice when I started talking about the biological control of weeds and my past work with the State Insectary. He'd been put reluctantly in charge of hiring a temporary weed specialist to map weed infestations in the county and make recommendations on weed control.

Weed control was a sufficiently unpopular and controversial topic in the environmental stronghold of Pitkin County that nobody wanted to be associated with it even from a hiring point of view. Mark, the environmental coordinator in charge of hiring this position, wasn't thrilled with his involvement in this situation and clearly, his heart wasn't in it. He'd obviously not even read my resumé and was surprised when I started talking about weed-eating weevils and caterpillars. By the time he heard about my own personal Painted Lady butterfly population, I knew I had the job.

Mark now had the opportunity to transform the lose/lose option of involvement with chemical weed control to the win/win heroism of changing the conversation from herbicides to butterflies. Even though I was up front with Mark about the inevitable limited use of herbicides in my eventual recommendations, he knew he could slip away in the chatter of butterflies and biological control vectors and distance himself from me before I got down to the dirty business of actually eliminating weeds. It turned out that there wasn't enough time for Mark to distance himself from me, but he was otherwise protected by diversion while the wrath of the entire environmental community was focused solely on me.

In the mid-eighties, when even a major resort like Aspen still had an off-season and became a sleepy little town with too much time for gossip during summers, weed control was one of the hottest, most controversial topics in town. My first assignment was to go introduce myself to the local press and give them a little interview. While they seemed interested in my experience with insect weed-eaters and my emphasis on non-chemical alternatives for weed control, the reporter covering the story turned out to be one of the anti-weed control extremists and was only looking for material to help rile up the environmentalists to eliminate my position.

The next day, my close-up facial photo occupied the top half of the front page of the *Aspen Times* with the subtitle: THE CHEMICAL COWBOY COMES TO TOWN! This was followed by a story talking about the county's new "hired killer" and the folly of giving the government money for poisons to spray on its citizenry. It wasn't a very popular or positive start, and I soon met out-of-state members of NCAMP (National Coalition Against Misuse of Pesticides), as well as members of CCAP (Colorado Coalition Against Pesticides), the Colorado State Environmental Coordinator (invited by CCAP), the lieutenant governor of Colorado (also invited by CCAP), members of the Northwest Colorado Council of Governments, and many other environmental and governmental sorts as well as scores of local activists.

I eventually managed to win over most of the opposition to weed control by trying to address all their concerns and by convincing them that I would run the most environmentally sound weed control program possible. And while I did apply some herbicides in a very low volume and selective fashion, I also continued working with weed-eating insects and purchased a goat herd for the County that we loaned out to ranchers primarily for the suppression of leafy spurge.

What spraying I did was conducted by hand on foot, so that weeds could be targeted very selectively, very close up without the overspray that would result from spraying over a distance from a truck. I developed a pack saddle spray system using a small 12-volt pump with rechargeable dry cell batteries. The sight of my mules and me walking the county roadway ditches and our goats out in the pastures became pretty popular with folks stopping to take pictures. I won a national award from *Better Highways* magazine for Excellence in Roadside Management.

With all the attention we were getting, Pitkin County's public works director decided we needed to formalize the use of my mules through some sort of contract or reimbursement arrangement. This proved to be very difficult to accomplish within the County's procurement policies. We couldn't classify them as contractors or pay them as employees without proper ID requirements, and we couldn't reimburse for mileage without a Vehicle ID number, so we finally created a new budget category called reimbursement for "muleage," and once again my critters were earning a wage.

In addition to earning wages, my mules also started earning wagers. Mule racing was becoming popular in those days, and I couldn't resist giving that a try.

Mule Racing

As a young wrangler, I'd been inspired by tales of an old horse trader with a fast, white mule. Horse owners can be as bad as fishermen about bragging and exaggerating, so this old horse trader would wait for someone to brag up their fast horse in front of large crowds before saying, "Shoot, I got an old pack mule can outrun that worthless nag." Having bragged himself into a corner, the horse owner was easily pressured into a high-stake race, often with several buddies anxious to place their bets too. The mule owner only raced for high stakes and only with small crowds in order to avoid a reputation that might scare off future suckers. Many small-time horse racers are secretive about their fast horses, changing names at every race and keeping their horse out of sight, or even disguising them with dyes so others will continue to run and bet against them.

Training any animal for racing can be tricky, but mules present exceptional challenges. And racing shouldn't be taken lightly as it often ruins critters for anything else. Racing can be addictive and often creates uncontrollable runaways. Long before the troubles with hot-rodding Dad's car around town was the problem of racing Dad's horse. Soon, any crowd of horses looked like a starting line and Dad's horse would take off like a streak of lightning through a crowd at the church picnic. I got in trouble racing wife

Kathy's mule, who started bolting like a streak of lightning whenever approached from behind.

When training, it's good to run with fast animals, but bad to be defeated too often. My friend, Paul, had a fast mare that my mule, Huey, was attached to and would try hard to keep up with. We lined them up on an abandoned dirt airstrip with a half-mile straightaway. Paul took off and established an early lead but, much to our amazement, Huey soon passed him up with ease. After a couple hundred yards, Huey started looking back over his shoulder and, after he figured out that we weren't being chased by anything, he slowed down. He'd just assumed that for a horse to take off like that, there must be something pretty scary chasing us. While he did have his moments, I don't think he ever ran that fast again.

I had a couple other mules, Fart Blossom and Duley, that I was also trying to train to race in the upcoming Garfield County Fair mule races. Huey was by far the tallest and most athletic-looking and was bred from a fast Quarter Horse mare, but his speed on any given day was subject to mood, racetrack, weather, fellow racers, astrology, and any number of other ill-defined factors. Whichever mule I was riding usually beat the other two, but nothing was very consistent and I didn't want to get outrun by someone else on one of my other mules.

I decided to try a quirt (a short riding whip) to see if it might help speed Huey up. The first time I quirted Huey, he spooked from being touched on the rump and ran off the trail, trying to look back to see who was behind him. We almost made it back to the trail unscathed when Huey jumped an unseen ditch, putting me up into the branches of a thorny honey locust tree, tearing off most of my shirt and some of my flesh. I finally got Huey used to the quirt, not because it did anything to speed him up, but because it made me feel more involved.

The first race we entered was the quarter mile. There were twelve mules entered, and I was in the outside position. Lining up a dozen mules to race can be a ridiculous rigmarole in itself because they get so crazed about competing. This was made worse by a few owners who used amphetamines or sometimes injectable vitamin B12 to further jazz up their mules. When the race started, I quirted Huey and immediately got the quirt tangled in his crupper (the strap under the tail on mule saddles), so my arm was stuck behind me by the wrist strap. Distracted by my struggles, Huey loped casually down the track eating dust.

Right as I finally tore my hand loose, Huey realized he'd been left behind by everyone and took off like a bat outta hell. We started passing the pack like they were standing still and as we went by Blossom and Duley, they both peeled out of the pack to keep up with Huey. Soon, we'd passed everyone except one exceptionally fast mule named Rocket, who was so far ahead there was no chance of catching him. Coming into the home stretch, however, Rocket spooked from the shadow of a grandstand pole across the racetrack. With the combination of the shadow and the roar of the crowd at the finish line, Rocket whipped around and passed us going in the wrong direction faster than we were heading to the finish line. A couple other spooky mules turned and followed him, and a few others made abrupt right turns toward the gate where they'd entered the racetrack. I finished first on Huey, with Duley and Blossom close behind in second and third place.

Having done so well, we decided to enter the pack saddle and relay races even though we hadn't practiced for these and would be competing against horses. The pack saddle race involved starting in a sleeping bag, jumping out and running to the horses being held by a friend, throwing a riding saddle on one and a pack saddle on the other, strapping the sleeping bag on the pack saddle, swinging onto the riding saddle, and running a half-mile circular track back to the start. The horses were all high-strung racing horses and half of them spooked and got away as the riders ran up with their saddles and sleeping bags.

Not expecting to win anything, I went slowly, avoiding most of the commotion, and was the last one saddled and going. Listening to the announcer on the speaker, I heard as one after another of the other riders either lost hold of high-spirited pack horses, slipped pack saddles, or got clotheslined by lead ropes and dumped. After a litany of such disasters, the announcer paused and said, "It looks like Jim Duke and his mules are in the lead! They're the only ones left in the race!" I could hear the crowd laugh and roar from the far side of the track. When we finally loped across the finish line at least a minute behind all the other uncontrolled horses, we got a standing ovation.

The last race of the day was the relay race. Each rider had three horses. Riders raced the first horse around the half-mile track, pulled the saddle off and slung it on the second horse, made a flying mount on the run to circle the track again, saddled the third horse, and did the last lap. Once again, all the horses in the race spooked and got the best of their riders or lost riders to loose saddles and were, one by one, disqualified. This time, because it was three laps, we were several minutes behind what would have been the winner's time, but we still got another standing ovation.

I've won a few mule races since then, especially with Blossom in the Potato Days Bareback Bonanza, but never had such a clean sweep as my first day racing. I still have plans for the future. There's a wild ass in Central Asia, the Turkmenian kulan, that has been clocked at over 40 mph, a speed approaching that of good racehorses. The greatest challenge will be collecting semen from the fastest wild ass in Africa so that we can artificially inseminate a retired Thoroughbred mare. With the benefits of hybrid vigor, the offspring might turn out to be the fastest equine on earth.

While it's unlikely the Kentucky Derby will allow the entry of a mule, no matter how fast, mules are fortunately excellent jumpers. A little preliminary reconnaissance will allow us to jump the wall behind the starting gates, pass the pack from a late start, and then jump another wall to disappear, leaving the racing world wondering, "Who was that masked mule?"

Cro-Maggie

As my reputation as a mule man spread, I was often offered free animals from folks who had wound up with animals they were afraid of or otherwise couldn't handle, but wanted to find a good home for. While I've come across some good freebies over the years, that isn't usually the case. Most "free" animals are worth considerably less than they cost. Cro-Maggie was somewhere in between.

A friend had recently bought a small ranch property north of Silt, Colorado that had a molly living on the land. She apparently came and went as she pleased and was often seen on the county road. Nobody could get close to her and none of the neighbors knew where she'd come from. Out of concern for her safety, my friend had called me to see if I might be able to do something with her. She was a very tall, athletic-looking red molly, and I couldn't resist trying to befriend and train her. I also thought that if I could train her, she would be hard to beat in a race.

Blossom had proven to be a universal ambassador among equines and seemed to attract and buddy up with almost any horse, mule, or donkey. While she had a uniquely gentle and kind disposition and seemed to be removed from the usual pecking orders of horses, it might also have had to do with her light gray color. It's said that mules in particular are attracted to white mares. The famous western artist, Charles M. Russell, was known for accuracy in his depictions of the west. In his well-known painting, *When Mules Wear Diamonds*, a double meaning showing a pack string of mules with loads secured by "double diamond hitches," Russell shows the pack string being led by a white "bellwether" mare. This was a common practice among packers.

I left Blossom on the ranch overnight and when I called her in the next morning, she brought along the stray molly and led her into a small corral. I backed my stock trailer up to the gate, led Blossom inside, and then very slowly and cautiously (she could easily have jumped the five-foot corral rails) urged the molly into the trailer with her. Her large, powerful build along with her heavy, angular eyebrows reminded me of the pre-historic *Cro-Magnon* man. Thus, the name "Cro-Maggie."

Although Cro-Maggie was very frightened and nervous about her captivity and people in general, she was obviously a gentle soul without any sign of aggression. This, unfortunately, didn't make her much safer to try to handle. She was merely way too large, powerful, and unpredictable. She also demonstrated several types of nervous "displacement activities" that I'd never seen before and which made me as nervous as she was. When I would work my way up close to her, she would look me square in the eye and then blink in an exaggerated way, making a loud, squishing sound as she blinked. It sounded more than anything like someone stepping on a wet sponge and reminded me of strange cartoon characters from my youth. When facing a "flight or fight" situation, such as the first time I mounted her, she would repeatedly suck in her cheeks and pop her mouth open very loudly in a confused way.

On separate occasions, I called in my two best horse-training buddies merely to try to get a halter on her and maybe try to longe her a little. Most trainers would have roped her, hobbled her, and/or whatever it took to render her into submission, and that wouldn't have been unreasonable in her extreme condition, but I was committed to being patient and gaining her trust as gently as possible.

After running her in circles in my round pen, trying to wear her out enough to be able to approach her, we finally thought we could sidle up to her. As we approached, she spun and kicked with amazing speed and control, popping a quick and restrained rear hoof against Jerry's chest. While she could easily have punted Jerry over the corral rail, she'd delivered a calculated blow that didn't even push Jerry backward, but left a perfect red hoofprint on the center of his chest. End of training session.

A week or so later, I tried again with my other buddy, Mario, the best horse whisperer I've ever met. This session also ended with a kick that sounded like a martial artist "snapping" a punch, leaving a perfect hoofprint on Mario's undamaged chest. Although at a total loss as to what to do, I was now convinced that she liked me (I'd been closer to her in both instances and she'd chosen to spin to the other targets), and that she didn't want to hurt anyone. She could easily have killed any of us but had chosen her least damaging means of self-defense.

Out of options, I built an extremely heavy-duty chute similar to what they run bulls through at a rodeo and, leading Blossom through first to lure Maggie in, trapped her in relative confinement. Rather than blowing up and trying to escape as a wild horse might do, almost certainly resulting in injury, she remained calm, true to mule nature, staring at me fearfully through several squishy blinks. She allowed me to approach and begin trying to pet and soothe her while her squishing advanced to mouth popping. Even though she stood stock still, her fear was contagious and it was nerve-wracking working up to her head and slowly fitting a halter on her. I then cautiously opened the end gate and led her out, prepared for an explosion. Although her eyes were full of fear, she remained calm and even let me stroke her neck a few times before releasing her.

After several such sessions, I eventually saddled her, led her around the round pen for short periods, and then started ponying her from Blossom. While she could easily have flung both Blossom and me off the ground, she felt secure with Blossom and wanted to follow her. I'd run out of volunteers to help hold her when I first tried mounting her, so I snubbed her up to a stout post, where I carefully climbed on and off repeatedly on both sides before finally mustering the courage to reach forward and unlatch her lead rope.

I expected the worst and was preparing for the roughest ride of my life, but she just stood there. With gentle pressure, I eased her away from the fence, expecting the eruption at any second, but she remained nervously calm. Although she was at least ten or twelve years old, she'd obviously not been ridden before, at least not long enough for any training, but she tolerated my restrained pressures to move and turn. She demonstrated the attitude of one who didn't like the situation but wanted to keep the peace.

Maggie turned out to be a quick and generally cooperative, if somewhat reluctant student, but she never relaxed and enjoyed the ride. Other than a few wild bareback rides on an untrained jackass in my youth, I was rarely dumped by any animal, but Maggie had no trouble launching me into orbit when spooked. It only happened a couple times and was never done with malice, but occasionally something set her off and she just snapped. When it happened, it was like a knee jerk reaction that she simply couldn't control. It was always just one huge buck and then she would stop and not even try to run away.

She did run away with me once. Kathy and I were riding in Rabbit Valley, near the Utah border, on a windy spring day. Wind makes all animals uptight and edgy and it's not a good idea to work green-broke animals on windy days. In this case, we were both on fairly green critters and I was much more worried about Kathy than myself. But when the big gust came whistling through their ears, Maggie was the one who broke and ran while Kathy unbelievably managed to maintain control, exponentially more difficult when her mule's best buddy was leaving her in the dust.

Suddenly, the beautiful cactus blossoms and rocks and desert scenery in general lost all allure, flashing by at the speed of light. My normal reactions to a runaway would have been to try to turn her tightly into a spin or, if that failed, to egg her on until she was so tired that she wanted to stop. In this case, however, I was desperate to keep her on the trail to avoid all the prairie dog and badger holes and countless other death traps surrounding us. And I knew that this trail led across the dam of an old cow pond that had washed out, leaving a steep gully about fifteen feet across and equally deep, so urging her on wasn't an option.

To make things worse, Maggie had never been on this trail before and wouldn't be expecting this huge gully. She, being the tallest runaway I'd ever ridden, added considerably to the fear factor as I started watching for a nonexistent soft spot on which to bail out. I wasn't sure she could stop in time or leap across the gully, and I didn't want to find out from that viewpoint. As I leaned slightly forward to prepare for the jump, I miraculously managed to stay on as she pulled off an impressive skidding stop. If she hadn't almost sat down during that stop, I would have gone over her head into the gully.

After that incident, Maggie eventually started acting calm enough that I felt comfortable riding even with my young girls along. We took a family vacation down to Canyon de Chelly in Arizona to ride the beautiful canyon and check out the ancient dwellings. Rules were more casual in those days and, although they still required a Navajo guide to enter the canyon, they allowed us to ride in on our own animals. The guide rode in with us on one of our mules but then caught a ride back out on a friend's Jeep tour, leaving us to camp by ourselves.

It was early spring and we'd had a good snowfall that night. As it warmed up in the morning, the wash began to flow with snowmelt and our young girls of six and eight years old decided to go for a dip. They ran screaming, barefoot, and naked through the melting snow to splash around in the knee-deep icy water, and then ran back screaming even louder as a bus load of tourists rounded the bend into sight. I doubt those tourists had ever seen naked young girls running through the snow before and, because our camp was out of sight in the willows, I was surprised that nobody stopped to investigate. I have to assume the bus driver was aware that there were campers in that area.

The trip had gone very well and we were almost out of the canyon and crossing the wash for the last time when Maggie erupted and I was launched again. I'd never been thrown anywhere near that high before and was lucky to land in a perfect bellyflop in the shallow, still ice-cold water. Kathy and the girls thought it was hilarious and loved seeing "know it all" Dad, always lecturing everyone on horsemanship, getting so unceremoniously and comically dumped.

I didn't mind being their source of entertainment, nor did I mind the icy dip, but I was finally convinced that I would never be able to trust Maggie enough for peaceful family rides. Someone besides myself was apt to get hurt sooner or later. I was also very fond of Maggie and concerned for her future. I ended up giving her to an outfitter friend I knew to be gentle with mules, on the condition that he return her if it didn't work out, rather than sell her. Maggie turned out to be the perfect pack animal and was much calmer carrying a load rather than a person. Her weird eye squishing and mouth popping eventually ceased, but not before gaining the attention of the outfitter's daughters, who singled her out as a favorite. Last I heard, she was happy and well loved.

Zebadiah and Sexy

I eventually came into possession of two really fast mules. Not that I was shopping for fast mules, or even shopping for mules at all at that point. In both cases, I'd merely been trying to help some friends shop for mules. Because these friends weren't very experienced with critters but did have plenty of money, I took them to a professional mule dealer who had a connection in Missouri for well-trained mules that he sold for top dollar. Although these high-dollar mules were out of my price range, that is where I met my current mule, Zebadiah. He was a beautiful, line-back dun with striped legs and a very athletic build similar to my first-born mule, Gunther, except that he was calm and gentle and had a great personality. I fell in love with him instantly but, even as a yearling, the guy wanted well over a grand for him.

With my friends buying a couple of his top-dollar mules, I managed to talk him down a little, but still paid several times more than I'd ever spent on any animal before, much less an unproven yearling. I've never regretted it for a minute. He has been my best friend over the past twenty years and provides us with endless entertainment. He remains the most curious and playful equine I've ever known, always inventing games for himself and whatever companions are in his pasture.

If there is an open gate somewhere, he'll get one of his buddies standing on the opposite side from him to play "bite me under the fence," where he will start biting and nipping over the top of the gate and slowly work his way down through the rails until both animals are down on their knees, or even down on their chests, biting each other through and under the gate. If there's a lead rope within reach, he'll start a game of tug of war that also often takes them to their knees. If there are no saddles, bridles, or garden hoses to tear up, he'll find a stick or something to create a game. I've seen him holding a six- or eight-foot branch in his mouth chasing the rest of the herd around. He always creates some sort of game that enforces a mandatory exercise session, working everyone into a sweat on a daily basis. Folks always wonder how I taught him to fetch my hat when in reality, he taught me that trick. He loves to fetch and will retrieve almost anything I drop or throw.

He was a bit of a nuisance when he was younger for his habit of chewing everything up, untying knots, opening gates, and even reaching down to pull up electric fence stakes to lay the fence down for crossing, but he would rarely run off. Instead, he would use his freedom to come find me or nose around pack saddle panniers or tents looking for food or fun. He was also very fast and won a few races for me, but he was inconsistent in his competitive moods, often preferring, if allowed, to drop back and bite at the heels of the competition.

About a year after I got Zeb, I was helping the same folks find another mule so they could take friends riding with them. We went to see a different mule trader who was known for training his own. He had a beautiful, black-and-white paint mule that reined well and even did sliding stops and such, but was nervous and high strung. We looked at a few of his mules, all of whom were well trained but also nervous. None of them seemed to enjoy what they were doing and I could tell the trainer was a little too heavy-handed.

While he was showing off another mule, a beautiful, blue roan appaloosa molly came over to check me out and make introductions. The owner told me she was only two years old and he hadn't worked with her yet, and he tried to redirect my attention back to his trained, high-dollar mules. I remained focused on the young, untrained, but much more relaxed appaloosa and asked if she might be for sale. The owner/trainer came over to where she stood calmly, enjoying having me scratch her chest and neck. Although she seemed trusting enough that I could have slowly worked up to haltering her, the trainer surprised both of us by trying to suddenly sling a lead rope around her neck to catch her. Unsurprisingly, the little molly spooked and dragged the large man across the corral before spinning around to sling him off and easily clearing the five-foot rail fence to disappear across the field at incredible speed.

I took advantage of the man's anger and frustration to negotiate a deal. Through heavy breathing, he sputtered that if I could catch her, he would take $500 for her. I immediately accepted his price on the condition that he allow me a day or two to catch her and let me leave one of my mules overnight to buddy up with her. My neighbors, having witnessed her wild escape, weren't so thrilled by the deal and expressed their reluctance. I reassured them that they could spend another few hundred dollars having my good friend and horse whisperer, Mario, train her and that she would be a splendid companion. Still uncertain, I offered to buy her for whatever they'd invested if they weren't happy with her.

The next day, I took Blossom over to spend the night and buddy up with the young molly. As previously mentioned, Blossom had the rare trait of being liked by all other equines. While generally the smallest and least aggressive of any given herd of animals, she was always instantly respected and followed as though she were the dominant mare. I'd used her in the past to help catch unruly animals.

Blossom's diplomatic abilities, already mentioned repeatedly, were truly noteworthy and transcended various species. Dogs weren't aggressive with her and, unlike most mules, she wasn't aggressive with them. I entered her in team penning competitions and she absolutely excelled. Team penning involves a team of two riders cutting three designated steers from a herd and moving them into a small pen. It's similar to a cutting horse competition, but on a much more amateur level. Blossom was so good primarily because she could calmly lope through a herd of steers without spooking or even upsetting them as we picked out and gently pushed the desired individuals from the herd. Most horses and riders put the herd into a panic. Cattle are much more controllable when kept calm.

At any rate, Blossom's diplomacy worked again and the next day, the young molly was easily persuaded to follow her into a horse trailer. Catching the molly, however, turned out to be the only easy part of working with her. She demonstrated the most extreme example of typical mule behavior in that she wasn't about to forget the sneaky rope incident with her former owner. That one brief attempt to deceive and overpower her dissolved any trust she'd ever had for humans, and I was also considered suspect by my association with the former owner. It required weeks of patient kindness to earn back any level of trust—an important lesson for any potential future mule trainers.

Sexy, as Mario had named her, eventually regained her trust in us and turned out to be every bit as wonderful and athletic as I'd predicted. She was, however, too much of a handful for the beginner owners she was intended for, so I ended up buying her as initially agreed. She was almost too much even for Kathy, a fairly experienced rider by then, but they soon established a mutual trust and strong friendship. Unfortunately, their working relationship was almost jeopardized when I started racing her.

She was a lot of fun to race mostly because she almost always won, but also due to the thrill of her contagious "do or die" competitive attitude. She had a very short, scraggly tail, which, as though part of her effort to put every ounce of her entire being into the race, she would spin wildly in rapid circles as she ran. Some of my competition almost fell out of their saddles laughing at this extra effort to give it her all, and I was often accused of cheating by using a propeller.

Sexy was not only very athletic but uncontrollably competitive. While Zeb was slightly faster when so inclined, Sexy was the better racer because she couldn't stand being outrun. The problem was that after a race or two, she couldn't control her desire to be out front. Anything threatening to pass her from behind would put her into an uncontrollable runaway. Not even a bird could pass by without triggering her competitive nature.

She also had incredible stamina and seemed to be an endorphin freak—fatigue seemed to energize her. I'd always believed that mules weren't subject to concerns such as running themselves to death, but with her I was afraid to even let her keep going, much less push her until she wanted to stop as was my usual practice with runaways. After a six-mile uphill run on a mountain logging road, she was drenched in sweat and lather and still pushing hard. I finally had to dismount to walk her out as the only way to calm her down.

I had to quit racing Sexy because it literally rendered her worthless for anything else. Mario and I decided to put her love for hard work to good use by training her to harness. By then, I'd acquired an old Amish buggy but had retired Blossom and had no others trained to pull, so Sexy seemed the obvious candidate and, for once, I had the chance to work with someone who knew how to train them properly. Mario trained Sexy and me together, working short sessions of an hour or less.

The first day, we fitted the harness and drove briefly in a round pen. The next day, we worked up to dragging an old tire around the pen and the next day, we put a bale of hay on the tire for a seat. I was finally growing out of my "on the job training" mode and was ready to learn the proper (and safer) techniques requiring more time and patience. This was also important because Mario had recently broken some bones in his right hand and I'd torn some of the rotator cuff in my left shoulder during a really good jump on my telemark skis followed by a really bad landing. Neither of us were in any condition to handle a full-fledged conflict with a healthy young molly. But on the other hand, we figured that between the two of us we had two good hands to work with and should be able to handle some slow and easy training.

Sexy was an excellent student and soon graduated to working outside the round pen on the open road. After a couple days of dragging the tire and hay bale, we figured she was ready for a buggy. Not willing to risk my expensive and delicate Amish buggy, we opted to pull my solid steel sulky I'd built years earlier to build fences with Blossom. Knowing it would be a little noisy on the washboard and chuck-holed gravel road, we figured that would help expedite her spook-proofing.

We let Sexy sniff around and check out the sulky while banging on it a little so that she would get familiar with the noise. We then hooked her up and headed down the road, still banging more than necessary to get her used to it. Our first outing went so well that we sort of let our guard down as we set out the next day. Things were going very smoothly until we passed a field of llamas who, curious about the clanking phenomenon approaching down the road, ran up to the fence line to check it out. Never having seen llamas before, much less having been charged by them, Sexy took extreme evasive action with her impressive speed.

I can attest that a runaway in a buggy is far more terrifying than a runaway while sitting in a saddle. This was further exacerbated by the overwhelming racket of the buggy clanking and banging over the chuck holes so loudly that Mario and I couldn't hear each other yelling as we fought Sexy and each other for control, each of us holding one rein in our respective good hand, as we careened toward a busy roadway. The image of crashing out into high-speed traffic was topping off our adrenaline rush when I noticed one last driveway rapidly approaching on our right. Shouting and motioning, I talked Mario out of the rein he was clutching so I could use full force in turning Sexy off the road and up the drive leading to a closed gate. Mario risked being bounced out of the buggy as he used his good arm to quickly cross himself in prayer before grasping the seat in hopes of making the corner. We almost tipped over before our sliding stop at the gate.

The very next day, I bought what is called a "forecart." A forecart is a heavy-duty work cart with large car tires and drum brakes. It has an equipment bar across the back for attaching various types of equipment for working fields. While a spooked animal could still drag it a ways, it was heavy enough to slow down and wear out a runaway when the brakes were applied. I would strongly suggest this sort of a buggy for anyone harness breaking an animal.

Jumping

I have several times mentioned the jumping abilities of mules. They really are excellent jumpers. A major difference from horses is that mules prefer to jump from a standstill and when they can see the landing on the other side. It's difficult to train them to take blind jumps on the run as is done in steeplechases. Mules are simply too smart, as well as having too strong a survival instinct, to take blind leaps. But once they have checked out the jump and landing, their abilities are amazing!

The first time I ever put Zebadiah into a closed box stall, I put him between two other mules he knew, so that all of them could look out the open top half of the stall doors and see each other. I was keeping my eye on them as I walked away. Zeb never showed the slightest sign of impatience or anxiety as he calmly flew over the four-foot-tall lower half of the door, gracefully sailing through the four-foot by four-foot opening of the top half of the stall door. It obviously hadn't occurred to him that the gate might have been intended as an obstacle as he trotted over to me, anxious to see where we were going next.

Family Life

Meanwhile, during my wildly up and down decade as an unlikely government employee for Pitkin County, I began to settle down a little into married and family life. I was a very involved father and had each of my two girls out mule riding while they were still infants in their "snugglies" strapped to my chest. When they were three and five years old, I packed Ellie and Emma on Blossom, opposite each other in pack saddle panniers stuffed with soft pads and sleeping bags for them to sleep on, eleven miles into the Conundrum Hot Springs above timberline in the Elk Range. For the most part, they loved all the riding and camping and adventures in general—but not always.

Jackasses and Traditions: A Muletide Story

It looked like a beautiful weekend with my only plan being to cut a Christmas tree. *What lucky kids I have to be able to join this greatest of all traditions! Wonder if I should try taking Emma along this year. I took Ellie when she was only two. Really not fair to let Emma miss out, but then again, be kinda tough handling both of them crossing the river—especially if I swamp the canoe or something.*

Meanwhile, Ellie practiced her five years of tact and diplomacy. "Dad, did you know they sell Christmas trees at stores?"

"Sure, why?" I replied.

"Well, all my friends get their trees at stores," Ellie suggested.

"Most people do," I explained. "It's more fun to go out and cut our own."

Ellie lost her composure. "I don't wanna go cut a tree! I just want to get a tree at a store like everyone else!"

I was devastated. Adding insult to injury, now I would have to buy a dead tree for ninety bucks.

The next morning, the girls and I went shopping for a live tree—the compromise to my quandary. Something to plant next spring. After a few minutes of checking out the larger than expected root balls and price tags, I started to question the whole notion. Then Ellie spotted some little spruce trees in one-gallon pots. "Daddy, let's get a baby tree!" What a perfect solution! Christmas is just for the kids anyhow, so as long as they're happy...

Back at home in the living room, I couldn't help but notice the several bushels of ornaments strewn about. A note on the counter informed me of an impromptu tree-decorating party planned for that evening. I was running out of time to go get a real tree.

The traffic was getting bad as I headed to the grocery store rumored to have $20 trees. Pulling into the parking lot, I encountered an impenetrable wall of cars and people probably all there for the same reason I was. This was ridiculous. I could go cut my own faster than we would get through these lines. I could maintain tradition by myself!

It was beginning to snow as I sped home spurred by the setting sun. If I really hustled, I could get across the river and find a tree before dark. Skidding a tree home after dark with a good mule would be no problem.

As I went out to call Huey in, I remembered that all my saddles and other tack were still at my brother's place from hunting season. No problem. I could just tie some reins on a halter and go bareback. The only rope I could find was a 1/4-inch poly rope. I hate that stuff. It's kinky and tangly and stretchy and yellow. There's nothing good about it. I started to consider the difficulties of skidding a tree holding a slippery, 1/4-inch rope riding bareback with nothing to snub to. *What the heck, I'm burning daylight, and that's just a detail to deal with later.*

Across the river, I followed the railroad tracks down about a half mile, where a recent slide had left several nice trees hanging off the edge and not long for the world. I try to be environmentally sensitive in my harvests from nature, so taking a doomed tree and the idea of being able to drop one right down to the tracks instead of skidding through the woods in the encroaching darkness made sense.

At the bottom of the slide, I tied Huey to a sapling and found a route to scramble up to the trees. I quickly cut a nice tree and was scrambling back down when I slipped and lost hold of the tree, which started rolling across the slope right at Huey. Huey, having never been attacked by a tree before, spooked and took off down the tracks dragging the sapling he'd been tied to. Much as I hate it, it's amazing how strong that poly rope is. After a short run, Huey was anxious to return for help, comforting, and the removal of the tree he was still dragging around.

Having now been chased by two trees, Huey wasn't thrilled about approaching the first one that had attacked him. I calmed him down enough to jump on and wrap the rope around my waist, but when the tree started following him again, I had to drop the rope to prevent a runaway. After a lot of dancing around and almost getting dumped a couple times, it became obvious that it would be easier to just walk home dragging the tree and leading Huey than to continue efforts to reason with him in the darkness of a developing blizzard.

Because Huey wouldn't get close enough to the tree to allow me to grab it by a branch while holding his make-shift reins, I was forced to pull it by the poly rope and endure the discomfort of the polyurethane rope digging into my shoulder, thus allowing the tree to follow at an acceptable distance while Huey stumbled along the tracks ahead of me, walking backward and sideways to keep his eye on the enemy tree. My spirits were beginning to dampen by the time I reached the river crossing.

Although I could see the warm lights of my living room across the river flickering through the driving snow, this promised to be the longest leg of the journey. I put the Christmas tree in the calm water at the river's edge planning to grab the rope from mule back on the way by. I coiled the rope and hung it on a handy branch hanging over the river so that I could grab the coil as I passed by. I would then play

Photos

Visit **wbp.bz/DWDGallery** to see the
following photographs in color.

Toilet Paper Race at the Bareback Bonanza, 1987.

Two-year-old Ellie riding Pokey, 1990.

Ellie on Blossom, Emma on Huey, Jim on Duley
during the Potato Days Parade, 1990.

Kathy packing elk up Capitol Creek in
the Elk Range Mountains, 1997.

*Kathy at the base of Buckskin Pass in
the Elk Range Mountains, 1998.*

*Kathy offering Blossom water in Courthouse
Wash, Arches National Park, 2000.*

Jim's handstand on Huey, Carbondale
Potato Days Parade, 2001.

Ellie introducing Otto to Zeb around 2002.

Kathy, Belle, Woody, Duley, Blossom, Jim, Zeb, and Dannyboy crossing Willow Pass in the Maroon Bells Wilderness area, 2004.

Emma introducing herself to newborn Lucky.

Adorable baby face of Lucky, 2011.

Jim riding Jorgé, Paco in Jim's shirt, Otto, the short-legged Jack Russel, 2010.

Charro confidently riding Jorgé, 2013.

Jim riding Jorgé, Emma on Lucky, 2014.

*Blossom enjoying a beer, possibly her
last, near her 38th birthday, 2015.*

*Jim proudly waving the flag on Zeb during the
Fourth of July, with Charro in pursuit, 2019.*

*Emma proudly displaying a string of
brookies caught on Zeb, 2019.*

Zeb retrieving a hat, 2020.

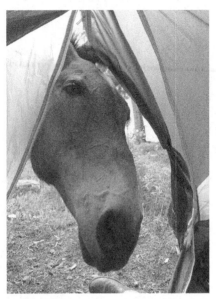

Zeb eager to enter a small tent at Navajo Lake, San Juan Mountains, 2021.

Lucky resting in camp, Vallecito Creek, 2022.

the rope out so I wouldn't have to pull the tree while Huey was fighting the worst part of the current. Then we would drag the tree across after he got good footing in the shallows on the other side.

But that's not the way it went. Wary of the attack tree lurking in the shallows, Huey covered the first ten feet in one leap. My effort to grab the coil of rope with frozen hands during this wild leap resulted in sticking my hand through the coil and getting securely tangled on a short leash. This put the tree back on the attack sooner than anticipated, thereby putting Huey on a much more dramatic retreat across the river. Unable to free my right hand tangled in the coils and being dragged backward off Huey, I tried to roll off to the side to land on all fours. That's when I discovered that my other hand had become tangled in the kinked-up polyurethane reins. I found myself hanging off Huey's side sort of pretzel-shaped with my left hand between my legs tangled in the reins while my right hand was stretched over my head tangled in the tree tether. In the blink of an eye, I was flipped, dunked, dragged, and dropped off in the shallows on my home shore side of the river.

I hardly noticed the icy water as I tried to count numb fingers with numb fingers in the total darkness. I was just starting to struggle toward shore feeling good that my digits were intact when I felt the poly rope tighten around my ankle. (Have I mentioned how much I hate that stuff?) I glanced back at the warm lights of my living room a mere fifty yards away through the driving snow as the tree entered the main current, dragging me with it. After a brief and futile effort at a three-legged, backward crabwalk on the slick river cobble, I realized that my only option was to attack. Swimming and scrambling in the general direction the rope had been pulling me through whitewater rapids, I quickly overtook the tree and began wrestling it toward shore.

Our company had shown up in my absence and my friend Jeff, having seen Huey run by in the light from the porch, was just coming out the door to investigate as I came trudging up from the river dragging my tree and a tangle of poly rope. He pretended not to notice my soggy condition as he dryly complimented the tree. "Sure is a big one. Not quite as nice as the one I just bought, but you did save yourself twenty dollars and the trouble of going to town and all."

Compost

Back at work, I continued to gain in popularity both with the general public and within Pitkin County and managed to expand my temporary position into a full-time one. I also began expanding the weed control operation into a more comprehensive land management program on the logical basis that timely revegetation of soil disturbances would prevent the eventual need for herbicide use or other, more costly weed control methods. I became a little more politically savvy and started using more progressively correct terminology, referring to being proactive instead of reactive and tuning in to the most current and constantly changing jargon so that I could sound cool and insightful in the endless meetings.

I also became too good at getting ahead of myself, something along the lines of the "Peter Principle," or always operating at a level above your maximum capacity. I was constantly throwing out wild ideas as though they were something easily accomplished or even something I'd done in the past and was familiar with. My previously mentioned pack saddle spray rig was proposed as part of my operations plan and was budgeted for, even though such equipment didn't yet exist anywhere outside my imagination. It's not as if I lied about anything; I merely failed to mention that much of what I proposed existed only in theory.

It was much the same situation when I first proposed using sewage sludge as a source of water, organic matter, and nitrogen for revegetation purposes. These were the three most limiting factors in plant establishment in mountain soils, and it's not as if this was a new concept. Folks around the world had been using human waste for fertilizer for thousands of years, albeit not without the risk of dysentery, hepatitis, and a few other concerns.

People in general don't like having changes imposed on them, and governmental bureaucracies tend to be even more protective of their own turf. Neither the Aspen nor the Snowmass Village Sanitation Districts wanted anything to do with me or my proposals. Instead of any sort of encouragement or positive feedback, I was handed a several-feet-tall stack of regulations pertaining to the land application of biosolids (sewage). It was obvious that regulations pertaining to slope, aspect, and distance to surface runoff and ground water eliminated 99% of the land in Pitkin County from potential application of biosolids. Both sanitation districts were rightfully quite happy with their current County-owned land disposal site located on some of the only flat ground in the county known as McClain Flats, where they dumped de-watered cake sludge into trenches for further drying and eventual burial.

Although it was a sound and affordable option for the disposal of biosolids, it struck me as a waste of valuable resources. Not easily put off, I came back with another proposal to compost the biosolids prior to using them for revegetation. The composting process provided sufficient pathogen reduction to eliminate most restrictions on application.

The sanitation districts were wise enough to avoid risking their irreplaceable disposal site to pursue some crazy cowboy's far-fetched delusions. They handed me an even taller stack of regulations controlling the composting of biosolids, and another yet taller stack of engineering specifications and recommendations for composting operations. To their satisfaction, I was sufficiently intimidated to finally give up on the notion of composting, although I suspected that the engineering specs were a bit of overkill for what was basically a natural process that should be much simpler than they made it out to be. One of the greatest obstacles in the regs was the necessary Certificate of Designation required for a compost facility. It was basically the same as, and possibly more difficult than, the siting of a new landfill. And this in the land where the term NIMBY (not in my back yard) was as popular as tree hugging.

Less than a year later, however, the poor folks living in the employee housing located near the McClain Flats biosolids disposal site started being displaced by a progressively wealthier crowd and soon, the sanitation districts were in court with some of the richest NIMBYs in the world. Apparently, someone must have remembered, "Hey! Didn't that weird cowboy guy want this shit?"

Before I knew it, I'd inherited the landfill, a non-compliant can of worms kicked around through Public Works staff, because that was the only site that could be permitted for composting. I was also told to waste no time in gearing up my compost facility, because I was expected to be able to process the majority of the county's biosolids in the near future. Be careful what you wish for.

Perusing through my mountains of composting regulations and engineering specifications, I was again appalled by how complicated and difficult this simple process had been made to be. The engineering specs, especially, made it appear that organic matter couldn't possibly merely rot and break down on its own without the aid of a certified, stamp-holding engineer. They required a very specific particle size of specific types of wood for bulking agents, and very exacting ratios of bulking agent to biosolids with tight tolerances on moisture and oxygen percentages. They'd made composting such an exact science that it was impossible to replicate it in a real-life, landfill situation. It was like the old saying: "Measure it with a micrometer, mark it with chalk, and then hack it off with an ax."

Having just completed my MOLO (management of landfill operations) certification, I realized that a primary challenge of landfill management was to try to prevent the mostly organic wastes from composting on their own after being buried. This sort of uncontrolled decomposition produces toxic leachates and excessive greenhouse gases such as methane. It seemed to me that I had an unlimited supply of bulking agent if I could simply separate it from the rest of the waste stream and grind it down to somewhere near the engineers' recommended particle size. I eventually figured out that the best use of all my engineering recommendations was as bulking agent in my compost piles.

As a life-long "trash merchant" and hoarder, managing a landfill, especially in the wealthy and wasteful community of Aspen, was like living in Disneyland. I was building my own home at that point in time, and I salvaged most of my windows and much of my lumber and other materials from the dump. I also quit calling it the dump or even landfill and renamed it the Solid Waste Center and Resource Recovery Facility. Knowing that the former landfill gatekeeper had been criticized for unfair access to all the treasures, and because liability issues forbid customers from salvaging among huge compactors with huge blind spots, I also started a public salvage yard. And because it seemed embarrassing that an environmental stronghold like Aspen had no recycling program in the late eighties, I started that too.

With the popularity of composting and recycling, my own popularity, which with the help of goats and mules was barely wavering back from my Chemical Cowboy days, also skyrocketed. Merely because most issues in Aspen received disproportionate publicity, these programs gained national recognition and won various awards and honors. I was elevated to almost celebrity-like status in a very strange and almost cultish way. It wasn't a very healthy thing, but fortunately it didn't last long.

I thought I was pretty hot shit traveling around the U.S. and Canada speaking about composting and resource recovery. Being slow in learning "no," I was soon booked with multiple local governmental agencies, schools, Leagues of Women Voters, gardening clubs, extension services, you name it. Suddenly, I had no time for myself or family or critters. I lived several steps from some of the best fishing in the world and never wet a line, was surrounded by the most beautiful mountains imaginable without entering them, and had the best animals possible just dying to hit the trail. I started seriously missing the solitude I'd given up. Being too well known and in demand can be worse, certainly more of a burden, than being the Chemical Cowboy.

I started basically dropping out of the scene, cancelling engagements, and just not showing up or spacing out appointments and such. At the same time, various hard feelings and ill intent started targeting me from within the county. Aspen has been described as a predatory community. There are lots of large egos vying for attention and many who don't like seeing others getting more than their share. It's a place to avoid letting yourself be put on a pedestal because there will be many wanting to knock you off it. I'd made a target of myself.

It must seem that I make a big deal about popularity around Aspen. One would have to be familiar with the weird Aspen social scene to understand such bullshit. There was a high society version of the typical mountain town "cabin crazies," where rumors and gossip can rule. While not important to most worker bees, anyone in a highly visible position with controversial or popular programs in their charge comes to realize that public opinion can either destroy or protect them.

One of the many lessons I learned in my many top to bottom, hero to zero cycles with the Aspen crowd was the fickle nature of false friendships. When a person is on top of the world, there are many "cling-ons" and groupies suddenly vying to be best friends. When the bottom falls out, these are the first folks to disappear. The message is that we only have a few real friends and that's all anyone needs. The fair-weather friends who come and go with the changing winds are merely distractions.

I started getting crosswise with the county manager, whose ego was tired of my elevated status. He approached me about appropriating landfill funds to be used on other projects. I refused to cooperate with compromising my successful programs to bail out his failures—I never was much good at dealing with authority. He could have made the change without my approval, but with all the press coverage I'd been getting, he would have looked pretty bad robbing from the county's most popular programs while highlighting the shortcomings needing to be bailed out. I'd become his worst pain in the ass and he made it clear that he would get rid of me any way possible. Even though I was more than ready to leave by then, I wasn't going to make it easy for him.

About that same time, my first marriage had just finished the final throes of a slow death and I became an accomplished barfly, demonstrating every aspect of the drunken, obnoxious, always on the make, worst case scenario of a recently divorced man. I entered the first real low point in my life. While I maintained a façade of decency in the presence of my girls in a half-time custody situation, I more than made up for it in their absence. Having been displaced from my beautiful log cabin I'd built on the shore of the Roaring Fork River and living in a spare room over the garage of my brother's house, I reveled in my misery at my favorite bar, the Ship of Fools. It became my residence to the degree that folks always knew where to find me and the service staff would take messages for me in my absence. The only inspiration I recall from that dark period was the following poem:

Ship of Fools

Just a mere inverted bubble
the disruption of an interface
And while not designed for trouble
the invasion of a fluid space
An experience most highly sought
when seas are resting quiet
An escape from always being caught
in life's inherent riot
But if the quiet lasts too long
and doldrums set the stage
We yearn to feel the winds rise strong
and waves of rhythmic rage
But then the seas become too wild
it seems that all is lost
More helpless than the smallest child
safe shores at any cost
But it takes more than fair-weather sailors
to guide this ship through life
Love beyond success or failures
devotion above strife
So, our voyage hasn't seen the worst
till love's elation slips
How easily these bubbles burst
to sink relationships.

Kathy

This dark period of my life began to change when I met Kathy. She was new in town and on a first date with a good friend of mine, Joe. When Joe had asked her where she would like to go on their date, she'd immediately responded, "Ship of Fools." She'd spotted this as a hotspot to be checked out but was still a little too proper in those days to enter such a rowdy place without an escort. Joe approved of this choice, noting that his friend, Jim Duke, would almost certainly be there and, it being a full moon, could probably be talked into a moonlit mule ride. Not surprisingly, he was right on both counts. Although I was with another woman, it was love at first sight for me, and I found myself wishing it was Kathy, instead of the other woman, who was clinging for dear life behind me on Huey as Joe and I took them on a wild run, riding double on bareback mules.

Kathy was a very respectable and successful mortgage banker at that point, and I knew I would have to make some major life changes to ever earn her interest. Trying to prove myself worthy of her became my primary life's goal. She was a sufficiently good judge of character that it took me a year or so to convince her I was serious.

Initially, she wouldn't give me her phone number and I was at a loss as to how I might ever cross her path again. Then, one afternoon on her way home from work, she saw me pulling my canoe up from a whitewater stretch of the

Roaring Fork. Dragging my canoe into the back of my horse trailer, I was shocked to have the girl of my dreams sneak up from behind and say, "That looks like fun!" She was still wearing the formal business type of attire common to the Denver area where she'd moved from. I told her to go change clothes and I would take her down the river. Although it was mid-summer with plenty of daylight left, I was shocked when she accepted the invite (challenge?) and even more surprised when she actually showed up at my house a little while later.

That whitewater experience led to some more mule riding and soon we became regular "play buddies," but she avoided anything resembling a date and made it clear she wasn't interested in any sort of relationship. But I had all the right toys and was more fun than her several other "suitors," so we wound up spending more and more time together, although never in public.

When I finally succeeded in talking her into going out to dinner, I didn't get off to an impressive start. Pulling up to her house in my beat-up old truck, I was surprised to see how nicely dressed she was and started changing plans on where we might go. Trying to compensate for my overly casual appearance, I escorted her to the passenger door to open it for her. Her tight-knit neighbors were apparently aware that she had a date that evening and all had found some excuse to be outdoors to check out her latest suitor, while I opened her door to release a cascade of beer cans rolling down the street. *Shit! Couldn't believe I hadn't noticed them before!* Things didn't get much better as I pulled away from the curb, throwing my young raven off balance and causing him to flap over onto her lap.

I'd hoped to impress her with this noteworthy pet, which I did, and after the initial screaming, they eventually became good friends, although she still to this day swears that she soiled her fine white slacks by sitting on raven shit, but Gabriel rarely shat anywhere except on the newspaper under his perch between the seats. That was our only "date" for a while.

Then one day, Kathy called to say that her brother was in town. He was in way too good a physical condition and had been kicking her ass in biking and other activities. She asked if I would take him bareback riding and hurt him enough to slow him down a bit. Her first wild bareback ride behind Joe had put blisters on her butt and left her sore enough to barely walk for a couple days. I complied and took Mark for a long bareback run—until he fell off and broke his arm. While nobody had intended any more damage than serious butt sores, Kathy got a reprieve from her ass-kickings, and Mark got a great story to tell and more female attention in the bars than he'd ever received before. Everyone was happy. Mission accomplished. In some weird way, this brought me into her family and opened the door for a more serious relationship.

The next time I finally talked her into another real date, I arranged to pick her up at the bank where she worked. I showed up in the drive-through riding Huey bareback. When the woman on the intercom asked how she might help me, I responded that I was there to withdraw a woman. After a long pause, she replied that I could probably have my choice. Right then, Kathy burst out the side door laughing and, without missing a beat, trotted over while hiking up her skirt (she's always had great legs and doesn't mind showing them off), grabbed my arm, and swung up behind me like a pro! We could hear cheering over the drive-through intercom as we loped off toward the Ship of Fools.

The Dance

I met her from a distance
While standing face to face
And thus began a soul dance
In the shelter of her grace
I felt an instant closeness
A connection from the start
And while I knew she felt it too
She kept our worlds apart
My life was then in chaos
My energies were low
While she was so well organized
And always on the go
Wise enough to keep her space
But strong enough to care
She slowly opened up to us
And all we had to share
And while it seems beyond my dreams
She's giving us a chance
And now the world is wonderful
And life is one big dance

Meanwhile, Kathy had encountered some very serious sexual harassment at a different banking office in Aspen. With both of us disgruntled and fed up with our work situations, we decided to just quit going to work and see what happened. For various reasons and weird circumstances, we made it for about a year with full pay before I was successfully fired (only time I've ever been fired and I enjoyed it immensely) and she was let go with generous compensation. In the meantime, we had a blast skiing, riding bikes and mules, rafting, and camping in the desert. We basically perfected the art of fucking off! We often tried to see how many different activities we could cram into one day. Her birthday, March 16, was the perfect time of year for the widest variety of activities. On her first birthday together, we skied, canoed, rollerbladed, biked, rode mules, drank heavily, and continued various other activities throughout the evening.

Kathy decided it was time for a vacation together. She was looking for an adventure and found one.

Cancun Honeymoon

I'd just popped another beer, trying to quiet the fungal alkaloids screaming through my brain, when we came around a corner to find a Federale roadblock of young guys with machine guns. Kathy was screaming, "Don't stop! I'm naked!" while I was shouting back, "I have to stop! They have guns!" We were still having this argument as I threw her my shirt to barely cover up with while I managed to get my shorts on as I pulled over onto the shoulder. I was tripping my ass off and the adrenaline started the whole world pulsating while lightning flashed around my peripheral vision as the Federales walked toward us.

It was actually more of a first date than a honeymoon and, other than the airport, we never did go to Cancun. I'd been pursuing Kathy hard for several months and, while I knew she liked me, she wasn't ready to admit that yet, at least not in public. I was pretty much your worst-case scenario of a recently divorced bar fly, far exceeding any standards of acceptable behavior. Kathy knew better than to hang out with the likes of me, but she also loved all the outdoorsy active stuff I was always engaged in. I was too much fun to blow off completely—as long as she didn't have to be seen with me in public. She probably decided to go to Mexico with me because she was pretty sure we wouldn't run into anyone we knew. That and because she'd recently read an article about "How to go to Cancun without going to Cancun" in *Outdoor Magazine*. It named some (previously) hidden secrets along 307 South toward Belize that she wanted to go check out.

We were 'shroomin our way down Highway 307, naked in one of those topless Volkswagens, engaged in most everything that shouldn't be attempted while driving, when we encountered the Federale check point. I'd tried to buy time to cover up by pulling over on the right shoulder across the highway from the wide pull-off to the left, where they'd been flagging me. As the Federale in charge crossed the road to approach us, I must have appeared as high and terrified as I felt because he stopped halfway, raised his arms, and said, "It's all right, I'm a Federale." He couldn't possibly have imagined how much that didn't make me feel better. I must have turned a whole other shade of pale because after two more steps, he stopped again and pulled out his badge and again reassured me that he was the law. Upon reaching our car, he leaned against the door to check me out and asked, "*¿Habla usted Espanol?*"

I was barely able to reply, "No." This was no time to practice my gringo Spanish.

Another officer who had approached Kathy's door looked at the beer cans on the floor, smiled, and asked, "*¿Habla usted cervesa?*" (Do you speak beer?) The first officer chuckled and asked me to pop the hood. While the second officer rummaged through our luggage, the first officer started looking through our stuff in the back seat. Those Volkswagens have a little glove box sort of compartment behind the back seat, where I'd originally stashed our drugs behind the carpet upholstery inside this box and then removed it, deciding it was too obvious a hiding place. There was now a bag of 'shrooms and a bag of joints under my seat in an even worse hiding place.

As the first officer looked through our stuff in the back seat, he casually asked me if we had any guns. I barely managed again to say, "No." As I watched him in the rearview mirror, he moved to the little rear glove box and immediately began looking behind the upholstery, where I'd initially stashed our drugs. He froze.

Shit!! Had I left something behind!? Was he about to pull out another bag!?

Without moving, he asked, "Do you have any drugs?"

I froze up, flashing harder than ever, my mind racing. *If he'd found drugs, the answer was "yes"; if not, the answer was "no"! Wrong! Think clearly, dammit! The answer is always NO!* But it really didn't matter anyway because I already knew we were going to prison. Some date! I was having visions of Kathy's Catholic and ultra-conservative college dean dad scowling over his shoulder at me as he bailed out his daughter, leaving me to rot in hell, where I so desperately deserved to be. The officer waited for my answer as my mind raced wildly. I waited for his move. Kathy waited for me to say something, her angry glare burning a hole in the side of my head like lasers. I could feel every fiber of her body silently screaming at me to do something. Anything! Say something, dumb shit! You got us into this! GET US OUT!

The Federale abruptly snapped the lid shut and walked back to the driver's door, leaning inward to look into my face and force eye contact. Sternly this time, he stated, "I asked you if you had any drugs!" Somewhere from the furthest depths of my being, a calm, level-headed observer rose to the surface. I found myself reaching for the beer between the seats, picking it up, and holding it in front of him. "Yes sir, I have alcohol."

He gave me a sort of scrunched up sideways look as if to say, "Is that all that's been bothering you?" He then turned and walked back across the road without saying a thing, followed by the other officer.

While I sat there in shock wondering if it was really over, a German hitchhiker who'd been watching with his girlfriend from a short ways off walked over and said in a heavy accent, "I tink dey done vit you. Can vee have ride?"

I said, "Sure, climb in." I felt my blood start to flow again. Just past the Federale roadblock, I turned left onto the side road leading to Mahahual on the coast. In Mahahual, we dropped off the hitchhikers and turned north toward Xcalak, the final destination of the *Outdoor Magazine* article. In those days, there was no paved road to Xcalak and the only way to get there, except by boat, was a three-hour rutted and potholed sand/rock double track barely off the surf. Somewhere along that coast we stopped for a while, a little ways past the middle of nowhere, with no sound but the ocean and no lights but the stars, and mellowed our mushrooms with marijuana. Without exchanging a word, we agreed we would spend the rest of our lives pursuing moments like this. We ended up buying some beachfront (mangrove marsh front) property in Xcalak and started an adventure that has continued for almost thirty years so far.

***

I also spent a lot more time with my two girls, having time to pick them up from daycare every day on my bike with a kid trailer, often stopping for a picnic along the river on the way home. Ellie was already well-advanced in riding Blossom on her own, and I found a beautiful little pony (technically a registered miniature horse) for Emma. Boonedocker, as we named him, was very gentle but completely untrained. He rapidly accepted saddle and bridle and never offered to buck or spook, but he was too small for me to ride. I'd seen other very gentle ponies turn into wild broncs when done the injustice of being mounted by an adult, so Emma was his first rider. At first on a short lead and graduating to a longe line, Emma and Boonedocker learned together. Emma can honestly claim to have broken her first horse at the age of three.

The three of us spent many a weekend riding and camping in the mountains and in the desert. Both girls had caught their first cutthroat trout by the time they were in preschool. We spent days wandering barefoot down desert canyons, with the girls catching tadpoles and crawdads in the wide shallow creeks. Desert canyons provided the world's best sandbox.

In many ways, my children raised me as much as I raised them. We all learn so much from our children. When I tried to cancel a planned camping trip with Ellie on a rainy Saturday, she, at the age of eight, scolded me for being scared off by a little rain. Embarrassed into compliance, we put on our slickers and rode off into a dismal drizzle. Riding in and out of fog and mist, we topped out above the clouds just below timberline on Mt. Sopris for one of the most beautiful, surreal views that most people never see. It was one of our most memorable trips, which we have always referred to as "cloud walking." I've rarely been a fair-weather participant since. In fact, as the Roaring Fork Valley became more over-crowded, we came to relish "foul" weather for some of our favorite hikes, knowing that there would be no crowds.

I also found time to spend alone or with my critters camping in the desert. Such trips were generally peaceful and uneventful but occasionally became somewhat of an adventure, often having to do with animals getting loose.

Justice Served in Courthouse Wash

It's not like I'd woken up that morning planning to be an outlaw, but I'd woken up to find my mules missing. Being camped on some remote BLM land above Arches National Park, I didn't think twice about putting on only my tennis shoes and hat and leaving camp in my underwear. There wouldn't be anyone out there that far from roads in the heat of late July, and I expected to find my critters nearby at the head of Courthouse Wash, grazing the rich sedges and cattails just below the spring located there. But their tracks indicated that they'd pushed under the PVC pipe flood gate designed to let flash flood debris through while keeping livestock out of the park. Still assuming they would be close by, I headed down the wash.

I hadn't bothered with a halter and lead rope. My mules all came when called, and I often rode my steadiest mule, Fart Blossom, bareback with no headstall. As previously mentioned, she was the first mule I ever owned and was eventually with me for thirty-seven years, making her my longest constant companion. I preferred riding bareback in those days, when she was still young and we'd come to move as one unit. I had good control without a headstall and would start many a morning on desert camping trips leading my whole herd on a several-mile wild ride with mules kicking and frolicking all around me while I often wore nothing more than my hat, skivvies, and tennis shoes.

The mules had gone on a good romp that morning, so it was almost ten miles later when I started hearing the sounds of angry shouting and squawking radios echoing off the canyon walls near the bridge over Courthouse Wash on the main road going through Arches. Although I'd walk/jogged as fast as the intense heat would allow, stopping only once for a drink at a spring halfway down, they'd already had enough time to call in the cavalry. As I approached the bridge, I saw two park ranger trucks and another truck with a big gooseneck horse trailer. One park ranger sat in his truck chilling in his AC and watching another ranger trying to disperse a gathering crowd of onlookers to keep traffic moving, his shirt soaked with sweat. Thus, I approached this busy scene wearing only my hat, briefs, and a bad sunburn, sorely wishing that I hadn't shown up so under-dressed for the occasion.

Anyone who starts out bossing and bullying a bunch of mules is almost sure to be starting a losing battle and is certain to wind up frustrated and angry. That is apparently what had happened here. I managed to slip past the rangers and under the bridge without drawing any attention other than a few tourists pointing from car windows. I soon came upon a very yuppie-looking cowboy on a beautiful paint horse guarding the wash above the commotion. I startled him from behind with a greeting and a compliment on his horse. Giving me a quick once over, he skipped formalities in telling me I was in a very dangerous situation and needed to return to my vehicle immediately. I then indicated his radio and told him that if he would call off his buddies for a minute, I could call my mules in.

"Your mules!?" He didn't wait for an answer as he grabbed his radio to excitedly report that he had the mule owner in custody and request immediate backup. He then started ranting at me about irresponsible ownership of dangerous animals and no, I couldn't help, I'd done enough damage already. They had the situation under control, and we were all under the custody of the federal government of which he was a duly appointed agent and on and on. I'd never had a total stranger so pissed at me.

As he continued raging, his horse and I were paying more attention to the crashing of underbrush approaching us through the tamarisk. I interrupted his rant to whistle my mule call and within seconds, Blossom came crashing out of the brush dragging a lariat followed by my other two mules and one donkey. Blossom was scared half to death and obviously glad to see me. The paint horse, already on edge from his rider's anger, was obviously not accustomed to the company of asses and started rearing and spooking backward into the brush as my mules rushed forward. I twisted the lariat on Blossom into a makeshift halter and was coiling up the slack when three riders appeared around the bend a couple hundred yards down the wash. When they saw us, they broke into a run, shaking out new loops and preparing for action.

This was crazy! My animals were standing as peacefully as possible in spite of the yahoo scaring his own spooked horse. These guys didn't want peaceful resolution. They were pissed and wanted revenge. They wanted to rope and choke down my best buddies! And the way they were thundering toward us, my crew was starting to spook and getting ready to run.

With rangers above and angry vigilantes below, I was struggling for a course of action when the pissed off paint owner, who had been forced into a most ungraceful dismount for fear of his horse going over backward, screamed, "Get your blankety blank mules away from my horse!" This not only sounded like a great idea but seemed to be a direct order from a self-proclaimed, duly appointed agent of the federal government. I shucked the makeshift halter off Blossom, hopped on, and hauled ass.

The first ranger (requested backup?) was walking down the drainage ditch and had no time for talk as he dove for cover from my little stampede. The second ranger, who had been on the bridge with his radio when we rounded into sight, had plenty to say as he ran, stumbled, and tumbled down toward the wash. "Halt! Stop! You're under arrest! This is evasion! Don't make it worse!"

I replied with, "Look out! Can't stop! Out of control! Call off your riders!" Pokey, the donkey, crow-hopped a few steps over and threw a side kick in the direction of the ranger to punctuate the end of our conversation, and the race was on.

Looking back over my shoulder every few seconds, I saw the three riders coming under the bridge with the paint horse guy close behind. Over the first half mile, the riders slowly closed the gap to within about fifty yards, but I wasn't too worried. Although Blossom was barely thirteen hands and built like a pregnant guppy, she was deceptively fast. Those riders all had thirty to forty pounds on me, not including their heavy western saddles, and it was at least a hundred degrees out. With Blossom being half Arabian and half ass, I knew I had the best combination of desert equines under me, and I'd not yet asked her for speed. Nonetheless, just for safe measure, I took a shortcut across a long meander on an ill-defined game trail I'd taken on the way down the wash following the mules' tracks, so I knew they were familiar with it too. I was risking a little sunburned flesh in the tight brush, but Blossom was best in tight quarters and any followers on taller mounts would have to dismount to negotiate some low-hanging cottonwood branches along this trail.

I came back out into the wash with a minimum of scratches and no pursuers in sight as I continued upstream. Soon the three riders came around the bend in the wash, whipping and spurring harder than ever, but two hundred yards farther behind and slinging lather with every stride.

Blossom was barely starting to sweat. Then the paint came crashing into the wash from the game trail, taking the lead of the posse but missing his rider, now replaced with the remnants of cottonwood branches hanging from the saddle horn. Guess that guy had been right about this being a dangerous situation. Rounding the next bend, I lost sight of my pursuers but let my gang keep running. They were still frolicking.

A couple miles farther up the canyon, my animals had slowed to a casual lope and I finally persuaded Blossom down to a trot and then a full stop at the end of a several-hundred-yard straight stretch, where I sat watching for pursuers and pondering how this style of briefs had come to be known as "jockey shorts." Obviously, I wasn't alone in my taste for riding apparel.

Two riders on spent horses trotted into sight down the canyon, where they stopped and sat glaring at me. I doffed my hat and waved it at them in the classic cowboy "*adios amigos*" fashion, to which one responded by raising his hand in what I had to guess, at that distance, was a less amiable gesture. I then gave my best "yee-haw," and for the first time that day asked Blossom for some speed, which she happily delivered, almost squirting out from under me as we zipped around the next bend and out of sight.

Xcalak

Having bought the property in Xcalak, Kathy and I started planning our adventure to build our tropical dream home, where we planned to live during winters, returning to Colorado during summers for what we envisioned to be a seasonal compost operation. Along with my girls (slowly becoming "our" girls), we would become fluent in Spanish and live in the best of both worlds. We did our best to plan for a huge expedition, loading my truck with everything we thought might be necessary or useful, and headed out to drive across Mexico.

The drive down was wonderful, and it was fun getting to know the people and the area, but it was the worst time of year to take on the huge project we'd set before ourselves. Our naivety in packing all the wrong sorts of stuff was almost comical and the heat and bugs almost unbearable. We'd planned to have my former wife and her new boyfriend fly down with the kids after we'd been there several weeks, giving us time to set up a more comfortable situation for three- and five-year-old girls. The onslaught of mosquitos during the summer doldrums without the steady sea breeze to keep them at bay necessitated the renting of a camper trailer to protect the girls from the elements, especially after Kathy got stung by a scorpion climbing into her sleeping bag.

All in all, it was a very tough summer and it's amazing that our budding relationship survived it. It turned out that the Xcalak region was basically the "Cajun country" of Mexico, with Mayan and French creole tainting their Spanish, rendering it a poor place to learn the language. This region was also heavily impacted by the drug trade and would probably never be a safe place for the girls to freely integrate with the local culture. We wound up leaving sooner than planned, deciding that, although it might remain a vacation retreat for ourselves, this would never be a second home for our children.

We did a lot of diving in the crystal waters off the coast of Xcalak and shared countless adventures and challenges in our times spent there, but we slowly came to realize that, other than diving and fishing, this region was mostly just flat scrub jungle and swamp with a few cenotes but otherwise not as diverse and interesting as most of the rest of Mexico. We eventually sold out and spent time exploring other parts of Mexico. One such trip was a surprise birthday present, where Kathy did all the packing and wouldn't tell me where we were going until we got to the gate at the airport.

Rodeo Clown

The big screen at the bar was showing the National Bull Riding Finals. It was there I witnessed the most graceful and athletic move I'd ever seen. The rodeo clown (bull fighters, nowadays) jumped up on the fence half a step ahead of the bull and tucked his hips in barely enough to avoid the bull's raised horns. As the bull passed, the clown, still carrying the momentum of his first leap, spun off the fence in a perfect pirouette to land squarely on the bull's back, where he rode with outstretched arms, Oaxaca style, halfway across the arena before making a well composed dismount.

I've always admired rodeo clowns and had aspired to be one myself. I've always preferred "rodeo clown" to "bull fighter" because I place more value on humor than on toughness. I suppose they changed the terminology to emphasize the danger and bravery over the humor, although I still wonder what sort of audience might ever have missed any of these aspects in the first place. What could be braver than making fun of that sort of danger?

I used to practice my rodeo clown moves while working cattle as an aspiring young cowpoke. The Black Angus breed I worked with in Iowa during my high school years often kicked, but rarely charged, and provided little training. But that all changed when I got to Texas and started working with Brahman crossbred range cattle. These were much wilder and more athletic critters, able to spin like a cutting horse and jump a four-rail fence. Most of them also had horns for better protection against coyotes and wild dogs on the open range. Most of those old girls weren't too impressed by a cowboy with a buggy whip and would rather charge than run away. That's where I got my clown training.

When we had a really wild-eyed, snorty maverick of a cow who was obviously not going to run through the stock pens willingly, I would dash across in front of her, right under her nose, to get her chasing me. With mad mamma hot on my heels, I would run through the chute, always close to the fence and ready to jump. Cows will almost always stop and plant their front feet prior to trying to hook their target with their horns, thus giving their target (me) an extra split second to hit the fence. Bulls, however, generally don't stop to plant their feet, but instead ram through any obstacles, slinging objects like slow cowboys and weak fences into the air like confetti as they pass through. For this reason, bulls require an altogether different approach.

The main rule with bulls is to avoid pissing them off in the first place. These are the ones to patiently baby along and try to make friends with. If you do upset a bull, running away might not work as well as it does with a cow who will plant her front feet and give you that extra half step. Bulls will outrun a person on a straightaway and not stop when they catch up. It's better to dodge and run past a bull, forcing them to spin around in order to continue the pursuit. Keeping them turning prevents them from building the momentum to overtake you.

It was less than a month after having watched the graceful rodeo clown spin off the fence onto the bull that I had a chance to practice my clown maneuvers. Kathy had bought us a surprise trip to Mexico for my forty-seventh birthday present. We spent the first night in old town Puerto Vallarta, in a beautiful old motel dripping and dropping ripe mangoes in every direction. The next day, my birthday, we rented a car and headed south. Late afternoon found us a little south of Barra de Navidad, passing through a small village with a celebration going on. Of course, we had to stop and check it out.

It turned out to be a bull riding festival. While this was our first such event, we have since been to several of these celebrations, which seem to happen in most small agricultural communities a couple times a year when they work their cattle spring and fall. Much like the fall roundups of so many U.S. ranches that have become large community events including barbecues and picnics, Mexican roundups are huge social events. Some communities have permanent corrals and arenas for these events and other communities, like the village where we found ourselves, built temporary corrals, usually in the village soccer field.

As we worked our way through the crowd, it became apparent that we were the only gringos around, causing us to draw a lot of attention. Most of this was a hospitable and welcoming sort of attention, but I couldn't help noticing that the older *vaqueros*, the most genuine of the cowboys, seemed a little put out by our presence, as though we were somehow desecrating something so special, almost sacred, to them. I considered turning back and leaving out of respect for these guys, but we were soon swept into the action, with enthusiastic hosts showing us around the food and beer vendors and setting us up with prime seats on the toolbox of a pickup parked against the riding arena.

It appeared that anyone was welcome to try riding a bull, and apparatus was provided for different skill levels. Some more experienced riders had regular bull riding rigs like those used in U.S. rodeos. There were also bareback riding rigs like those used on horses for bareback bronc riding and a variation of those rigs that had two handles instead of one for beginners wanting to hold on with both hands. Both these rigs were considered safer than the conventional bull riding rig because there was less chance of getting the riding hand stuck in the rigging. Let go of the handles and you should fall free. The problems arose because these rigs were connected solidly to the bull by a cinch that didn't release when the rider fell off. While not usually a problem, there were a couple guys who got bucked off but got a boot spur stuck in one of the handles as they fell and wound up hanging by their boot heel upside down off the side of a bucking bull.

Other safety problems arose from the makeshift nature of the loading chute and swing gate. A bull would be crowed into a small chute, much like those used in the U.S., to get the rider mounted. But they also had a halter on the bull so they could snub it up to better immobilize it while loading inexperienced riders. When the rider was ready, timing became critical. Simultaneously, one cowboy would pull a slipknot on the halter to release the bull's head while another would swing open the gate as yet another zapped the bull with an electric hot shot from behind. This usually worked well, but occasionally the halter wouldn't drop all the way off and would snag the end of the bull's snout, snapping its head around against its momentum and causing it to flop over onto its side. A couple guys were injured by their bull flopping over like that and landing on the rider's leg.

After a while, one of our hosts asked if I would like to go look at the bulls in the holding pen. We walked over to the pen, where he climbed the fence and hopped in with the bulls. He was surprised when I did the same, so to further test my bravery, he asked if I wanted to try to touch one of them. I responded, "*Quiro montar!*" (I want to ride!). Because he spoke no English and my Spanish was poor, he clarified by reiterating "*¿Quires montar?*" (You want to ride?), while pantomiming the action of riding. When I confirmed, he got very excited, asked my full name (he already knew me as Jimé) and disappeared, apparently to find the announcer.

As I walked back toward Kathy, I heard my name being announced over the bullhorn as an upcoming rider. "*El*

Americano, Jimé Dook, va a montar un toro!" The crowd went wild over their first ever gringo contestant and I was locked in as a rider. When I got back to the pickup where Kathy was still seated, she looked concerned. "Did I just hear what I thought I did?" she asked. "Are you sure this is safe?"

I had to wonder what she'd missed from the scene we'd been watching. Several young men had been dragged from the arena, at least a couple with broken bones. "Safest bull riding I've ever seen," I replied. That much was true. The *vaqueros* seemed to be familiar with their animals and assigned them to riders accordingly. The older bulls known to be hard buckers were reserved for the more experienced riders. Younger, less experienced bulls were assigned to beginners. If bulls had horns, they were padded with old saddle blankets to prevent riders from getting gored.

They also had a designated rodeo clown as well as several other spotters in and out of the arena as needed to haze bulls and help riders escape. The older *vaqueros* on their dancing stallions seemed to be there mostly for show, but they were quick to enter the arena with their rawhide lariats when things got out of hand or when an unruly bull needed to be dragged out of the arena. Their skills were impressive and justified their pride. They again made me intensely aware of being an outsider, but they were now checking me out as a potential contestant, probably hoping their bulls would teach me a little respect.

As my turn to ride approached, some of the local organizers began to get nervous. They'd apparently assumed that I would back out and now that that didn't seem to be the case, they appeared concerned about the liability of risking the safety of a tourist. They asked if I really wanted to go through with this and tried to offer every possible chance to back out. They encouraged me to at least put on some long pants and boots, but I opted for shorts and tennis shoes since that was all I had. The guy with the bullhorn didn't share their reluctance and made a show of enthusiastically announcing their gringo rider.

My bull was a black one appearing to be of the variety used for bullfighting. They wrapped his horns in pieces of old saddle pads and got me mounted. They swung the gate, pulled the halter slip knot, and hot shotted the bull all simultaneously, but as the bull spun out of the chute, the halter caught on his nose, snapping his head back and throwing him on his side. I was ready for this and got my leg out of the way, but I stayed half mounted, assuming he would jump back up. But he'd hit his head hard on the ground and seemed stunned by the blow as he rolled upright, still on the ground with legs tucked under him and his head swaying around in a daze. The hot shotter zapped him again several times without reaction.

It became apparent that the bull wasn't getting up, but not wanting to waste my only bull ride ever, I started rocking wildly, flinging my arm over my head and yee-hawing at the top of my lungs like I was on the meanest bull ever. The crowd joined in and started cheering my imaginary wild ride with great enthusiasm. After a few seconds, I got "bucked off" and flung myself on the ground. As if on cue, the bull came to life, jumping up so fast I barely got out of the way as I scrambled back up on the chute. Recovered and angry, the bull chased all the spotters up onto the rails and came back and rammed the chute right below me, trying to get back into the bull pen. Unsuccessful, he then spun back around to face the empty arena with his rear end toward me. The vision of the graceful rodeo clown leaping off the fence flashed through my head and without thinking, I found myself flying off the fence to land squarely on his back. This time, the bull bucked for real, taking me halfway across the arena before spinning hard and causing me to bail.

My landing rolled me back to my feet just in time to face the bull as he turned to charge. My Texas cowboy training came back instinctively. Knowing I couldn't outrun him to the fence, I dropped into a four-point stance ready to dodge and run past him when he charged. This startled him enough to make him hesitate and paw the ground with the classic bull display. Not wanting to move until he did, I hammed it up a bit and started pawing the ground too, like I was also ready to charge. The roaring crowd fell silent, certain they were about to witness the gringo's gruesome death. But the bull's hesitation was just long enough for the clown to jump off the fence and run between us, drawing the bull with him.

Scrambling out of the arena, I was an instant hero with beers, tequila, and cigarettes being thrust at me from every direction. I was basking in all this glory and making plans to spend the night so I could ride again the next day. There was no lodging nearby, but we had many offers to stay with locals and I was rapidly becoming too drunk to go anywhere. Kathy finally got the chance to pull me aside.

"Are you really going to ride again?"

"Well, hell yes! The finals are tomorrow!"

"Stop and think about this for a second. Do you really think you're going to improve over what you just did? Maybe you should quit while you're ahead—and alive!"

I realized she was right. I thanked all my new hosts and offered regrets for having to run but let Kathy steer me to our car and drive us off. As we were leaving, the old *vaqueros* all went out of their way to make eye contact and tip their hats. That was by far the best approval I could have ever asked for.

***

Most of our trips to Mexico have been blessed with incredible hospitality and genuine friendship and kindness. This has always amazed me in light of the poor treatment so many Mexicans receive in the U.S. It has been very rare to encounter anyone south of the border who harbors any sort of resentment toward us as Yankees. One such encounter occurred when we were visiting my niece in Xico, where she'd moved with her twin boys and her husband from that region.

Running with the Bulls

What thrill seeker could possibly resist this opportunity? No, this wasn't Pamplona, Spain; it was the small town of Xico, Mexico. But the reviews and statistics indicate this bull running to be even more dangerous than the original event in Spain. This is mainly due to the fact that, unlike Pamplona, where they release all the bulls from the same place at one end of town so the herd stampedes through in a somewhat more predictable fashion, the bulls in Xico are released from portable chutes scattered around town so they approach randomly from many directions. This is exacerbated by the narrower streets, further narrowed by plywood walls constructed to protect business fronts while also allowing a protected zone for spectators.

The peaceful, spiritual, and artistic morning in this lovely village couldn't have stood in sharper contrast to the events to unfold later in the day. While the bulls had been delivered earlier and stood waiting in black shipping crate boxes around town, the streets were all decorated with beautiful "sand drawing" type artwork made with various colors of sand and sawdust, covering most of the streets in elaborate designs. It appeared that every church, business, and youth organization in town was involved with the artwork, being both cooperative and competitive. It was joked that everyone should view and appreciate the artwork quickly because the impending rainstorm was almost as reliable as the tradition of the art. And sure enough, as though on cue, late morning brought one of the heaviest downpours I'd ever seen and, like a short-lived butterfly, the beauty disappeared in seconds without a trace.

As the skies cleared, the streets began to fill up behind the protective barricades with the heaviest traffic in front of popular bars, people staking their claims to front row seats. Out in the streets where we bull runners gathered, some sort of local sweet cider flowed freely with toast after toast to the upcoming event. Being the only gringo in sight, I was repeatedly toasted and high-fived but, as one of the oldest runners, then in my fifties, I was also warned of the serious dangers involved and further cautioned that, once the bulls were released, the traditional custom was that runners weren't allowed to climb the barriers but were required, as enforced by the spectator crowds, to remain in the streets for the duration of the event.

After the lengthy "pomp and circumstance" that comes with all Mexican celebrations, the moment arrived, and the bulls were released. I immediately realized that my greatest danger wasn't the bulls, but the crowds of other runners. I was used to working cattle, including some pretty wild range cattle, in fairly small pens and alleyways, but only when I had room to dodge and maneuver. While I was mostly worried about drunk and/or inexperienced runners getting in my way, I was also keenly aware of being the only gringo involved and the possibility of being somewhat of a target. Although I've always found the Mexican culture to be very kind and welcoming, many have suffered various forms of prejudice and abuse north of the border and some, although surprisingly few, of those abused carry a grudge. This wouldn't have been a good situation in which to encounter someone wishing me ill.

There was quite a thrill as the first bulls ran by and runners tried to avoid horns, hooves, and each other in the commotion. Some had brought capes and wooden swords to engage in daring bull fighter demonstrations. Others tried to grab horns or tails in quick dashes past the confused animal, sometimes poking them with sharp sticks. Most just tried to stay out of the way.

I'd entered this fray without plans or expectations but soon decided that I would at least try to touch a bull, as that seemed to be the minimum goal of the more adventurous. Avoiding the more congested center of activity where bulls were being harassed from every angle, I focused on a bull slowly walking away from the commotion swinging his head from one side to the other in response to any movement that might threaten him from the crowds on either side. I'd stalked my way close behind him and was preparing for a mad dash in to push or kick off his ass when he suddenly dropped to his knees. Moving to one side for a better look, I realized that, in the middle of all this ruckus, he was trying to suck and lick water from a small crack in the pavement. The cruel revelation struck me like a ton of bricks, or more accurately, sharp sticks, landing squarely at my feet as one of the responsible parties. How long had these poor beasts been without water? And in the heat of those poorly ventilated black boxes? When had they been dropped off? At least yesterday—maybe the day before? How could I have failed to notice their situation? I was suddenly sickened by what I was involved with.

These poor creatures had been tortured into a state of rage! And in their state of desperation, they were being further tormented by people like me. I felt like I deserved to get gored and trampled, but instead I walked to the closest wall to climb out of the street. I was pushed back from the wall.

"*Quiro salir*," I said. (I want to go out.)

"*No se puede*," several responded in unison. (You can't.)

As per tradition, they weren't going to let me out. A couple bulls ran past, swinging their heads, looking for targets. I froze along with the rest of the crowd lining the perimeter. After the bulls passed, I began working my way back to the bar where I'd entered the street and where the rest of my family was seated so I could remove myself from this inhumane situation. Up ahead, I saw four bulls walking abreast coming my way, moving warily, watching for threats and ready to charge. Nobody wanted to get in the middle of four bulls, so the crowd was surging in my direction. Meanwhile, two other bulls approached from the other direction, trotting toward the four abreast, occasionally lunging at the crowd. The convergence of these six bulls created quite a cluster along the perimeters on both side of the street, and I found myself on the edge of the throng closest to the bulls, with people crowded five or six deep behind me against the wall. We were all frozen, practically holding our breaths, hoping not to disrupt the bulls in this crowded situation.

Even the spectators behind the barricades had fallen silent, and you could have cut the tension with a knife when I heard some subdued snickering, mumbling, and made out the word "*gabacho*" just behind me. I looked over to see several Mexicans looking away, looking down, looking anywhere but at me. The term "*gringo*" is mildly derogatory, usually in a joking fashion. *Gabacho* is considerably more derogatory, especially when directed at a stranger and in a subversive manner. I glanced back again and noticed one of them had moved a little closer and met my glance with an artificially friendly smile. This was the guy I'd hoped not to meet.

I returned his fake smile, adding a wink, and inclined my head toward the bulls with a nod to signal, "Let's go. I'm ready. Are you?" I'd turned sideways, half facing the bulls and half facing the crowd and this guy, ready to grab anyone thinking about pushing. While never having been any sort of "tough guy," I'd been a good wrestler in my day and was still active in martial arts. I was confident that, if anyone tried to shove me, I could make sure they wound up between me and the bulls. I maintained eye contact as his smile slowly faded and he finally looked down.

The two more aggressive bulls had turned around again and all of them continued up the street beyond my location. When I finally made it back to where I'd entered the street, my friends and family helped pull me over the barricade, glad to see me alive and eager to hear about the adventure.

"How was it?" I was asked.

"Well," I said. "Not as much fun as I'd hoped."

***

We also occasionally flew down to Mexico in our own little Cessna 182. Way back during my lost and wandering college years, I'd taken out an emergency student loan to buy in on an old Cessna 152. I'd almost bought an old hang glider at a garage sale, planning to take it up to the hogback ridges west of Ft. Collins and teach myself how to use it. My girlfriend at the time had dissuaded me from the purchase and redirected my desire to fly by purchasing an introductory flight lesson for my birthday. A couple of my trucker buddies from Cactus Hill had recently bought the Cessna and offered to let me buy in. Thus, I had my first real plane before I had my first real job. It might not have been the most responsible decision, but it did lead to countless fun adventures.

A Bum In La Paz

The buzzard tucked into a dive at the last second as I simultaneously banked hard right, barely avoiding a direct prop strike. Damn! Didn't think an old buzzard could move like that. Many large birds tuck and drop as a last-ditch escape tactic. I made a mental note to NEVER try to fly under any large bird and removed my headphones until wife Kathy quit screeching into her voice actuated microphone.

Flying the Baja Peninsula of Mexico provides a great winter escape with a little added adventure. It's a bit edgy flying over the Sea of Cortez in a small aircraft because one should always have an escape route, especially in a single engine plane. But it's possible to fly high enough, theoretically, to glide to either coastline from the middle. The plane has a service ceiling of 18,000 feet, but it starts sputtering enough at 16,000 that I don't push it. Probably just as well, since this is already much higher than allowed without oxygen. But we spent a lot of time at altitude, and I considered the occasional screaming to indicate healthy acuity. Kathy, my canary in the coal mine.

I'd also studied water landings and had picked a course that passed two islands in route in case we had to ditch and swim. There's an abundance of info on how to survive water landings, but the bottom line is that tricycle gear planes like my Cessna nearly always flip over hard enough to knock everyone unconscious, so it's basically get ready to kiss your ass goodbye. At any rate, we'd made it across and had since made many happy landings on sand strips along the coast, some with Unicom radios, allowing us to have fish tacos and margaritas waiting at the end of the runway.

Even the easy landings usually involved dodging vultures, frigates, and pelicans. Although approaches often involve crossing the surf, the concentration of seabirds was hard to account for. The buzzards, on the other hand, were assumed to be there for the carcasses of other birds hit by aircraft.

Flying around Mexico isn't cheap. Well, flying in general isn't cheap, but we've always been comfortable living beyond our means and, with just a few poor decisions, almost anyone can afford to buy and fly a small aircraft. It's not a whole lot dumber than owning an average-size water skiing or fishing boat. As the saying goes, "If it floats, flies, or..." Well, let's just say that some things are cheaper to rent. Anyway, Mexico has many fees added to private air travel. There are landing fees, takeoff fees, flight plan fees, and other rather ill-defined fees, usually including a bribe to the ever-present military personnel on all airstrips. This can be a tricky sort of bribe because it should be enough to make them want to protect your plane, but not enough to make them abandon their post to go get drunk.

Having always been a thrifty traveler and speaking enough Spanish to usually banter prices down from the tourist gouging rates, it was a little painful getting accustomed to all the extra fees for flying. Like most tourists in Mexico, I relished the bragging rights on how cheap I'd gotten this or that. Flying around, however, was enough fun that it wasn't too hard to bite the bullet on all the extra fees—until we got to La Paz. Suddenly, it seemed that all fees were doubled. Things didn't improve much upon reaching the city. Meals, motels, and everything else cost almost as much as back in the U.S.

That evening, we were sitting at an outdoor restaurant patio, scanning an overpriced menu and plotting our escape to cheaper pastures when an older, rather unkempt man with long, gray hair sat down at the next table. He looked enough like a street person that I avoided eye contact.

He was soon joined by a young couple who were obviously happy to see him. After chatting for a while, the old man reached into a battered satchel and pulled out a folder. He started passing around some of the most beautiful artwork I'd ever seen. He had sketches and charcoals and watercolors of such quality that even I could see that this was a man of great talent.

After his clients left, the tables had turned and now I was hoping to catch his eye while he had every right and reason to avoid mine. When he was preparing to leave, I drummed up the courage to introduce myself. While I had little doubt that he'd noticed my initial reaction, he was, nonetheless, very open and friendly. He politely declined my offer to buy him another drink but didn't seem to be in any hurry to leave or do anything else. He was completely comfortable with any stretch of silence, but patient and articulate in response to questions.

When asked, he spoke of his decades in Mexico and of the many places where he'd lived. He was obviously well traveled, familiar with every place I'd ever been and many more. He had a gentle way of looking deep into a person without being invasive. As he took a sip of the melted ice in his tea glass and was again preparing to leave, I asked him what part of Mexico he liked best.

"Right here," he replied. "That's why I live here." He must have noticed the puzzled look on my face because he added, "Why do you ask?"

"Well," I said, "it's so much more expensive than the rest of the country."

He'd just stood to leave but sat back down. His eyes locked on mine again—benevolent but penetrating. Like he was inspecting the weeds and litter tangled in the farthest fence-lines of my subconscious. "I've noticed that the less expensive it is for me to live, the more suffering I see around me. I'd rather pay a little more and see others living a better life."

My self-esteem tucked into a nosedive, swooping down far beneath the soles of my new, designer flip flops. Damn! Outmaneuvered by another old buzzard! My mind jumped to my bumper sticker at home: "Everyone does better when everyone does better." It moved to a narrative by travel writer Paul Theroux, concerning rich tourists talking down prices at local mercados just for sport when a few pesos to the vendors might make a difference in how much their children ate that night. Sure, we can justify defending ourselves from the onslaught of scammers at typical tourist centers, but I'd crossed the line flying around looking for affordable Mexico.

As I watched him walk away, I realized that while I thought I'd introduced myself to him, he had, instead, introduced me to myself. And I can't say it was much of a pleasure meeting me.

The old artist had chosen to live in La Paz, which means "peace" in Spanish. I hope to live there too, someday, wherever I may find it.

***

Back in Colorado, Kathy and I were starting our new lives together. Moving back from Xcalak, we'd found ourselves broke, unemployed, and basically homeless. While Kathy and I both owned homes in the area, we had them rented out and couldn't afford to do without the rental income. I got a construction job and lived in my back yard in a camper while Kathy cruised and camped for a few more weeks until I could afford to take over the smaller of my two rental units. It was finally time for us to get back to work, and we were both a little concerned. Sure, we'd proven that we could play well together, but how would we hold up in a real life and career type situation? Were we destined to be only fair-weather friends? We decided to find out.

Wedding

It was sometime during our travels in Mexico that Kathy and I decided to get married. I'd long since purchased my riverside property and cabin back from my former wife, and that's where we tied the knot. We'd inherited a matched pair of miniature donkeys at some point and we'd named our property the Little Ass Pen in their honor. The little pair always walked side by side in unison as though controlled by one brain. We called them Daryl and Daryl. They were out by the front gate humping each other as guests arrived at our wedding. The Little Ass Pen has since held four other weddings, all of which are still intact and healthy at this time.

Our wedding was conducted in beautiful fall weather along the Roaring Fork River. Kathy made her entry on a lovely carriage pulled by a team of even more beautiful black Percherons, seated next to her proud father and serenaded down the drive by a two-man string band. Once they'd disembarked from the carriage, I made my entry along the riverbank from the opposite direction at a dead run on Duley, swerving, dodging, and weaving through the tables, chairs, and crowd.

As I approached Kathy and her dad, I heard someone say, "Oh my gosh! I wonder if he's going to stop?!" That struck me as an excellent idea and, rather than the planned sliding stop, we kept right on going, past Kathy and her dad, past the crowd, and up the driveway out of site.

Of course, I came back pretty quick and even Kathy thought it was a funny little stunt, but said she'd been worried about her proper and conservative father, who kept asking, "Kathleen, do you think he's coming back?" We had more fun than I think people are supposed to have at their own wedding, and that's been the trend for weddings at the Little Ass Pen ever since. Now all we had to do was figure out what to do with the rest of our lives.

I'd lost my huge operation with Pitkin County and all the glory that came with it, but I'd found my calling. I'd been fascinated with composting from the very beginning, before I even made my first pile. When I had my first pile heat up, I was absolutely hooked. Digging into that steaming pile and enjoying my first sewage sauna, I felt completely connected and grounded through my compost. It's as though I'd found something I didn't know I was looking for, but once discovered, I knew I'd always been seeking it. My attraction to farm and ranch work had been efforts to get closer to the earth. The source. Compost was my vehicle to become intimately immersed with earth processes.

I'd graduated from weeds, to trash, to sewage and couldn't have been happier. I'd come to view shit as the most under-rated but most important link in the great chain of life. It was the beginning and the end, the yin and yang of life. With all the talk about permaculture and sustainable agriculture, I was sitting on the cornerstone of sustainability. From that point on, my personal cause and my career became one in the same, which is about as much as one can hope for in life. I would have continued pursuing composting even if it had driven me into poverty. But against all odds, composting became very profitable for us. It was almost like a Paulo Coelho novel, where "when you are on the right course, all of nature conspires to help you along."

Due to over-grazing, tilling arid lands, and general mismanagement, our nation has lost most of its topsoil and its valuable organic matter. Organic matter acts as a sponge in the soil not only to hold water, but through electrical charges in the organic matter referred to as the cation exchange capacity (CEC), helps the compost bind to nutrients, such as nitrogen, and hold them to be released slowly as the soil microorganism die and decay, allowing the natural cycling of soil nutrients through organic matter.

Most forms of nitrogen fertilizer are very soluble or volatile, meaning that they're easily leached or off-gassed from the soil. Organic nitrogen is released on a schedule that mirrors the nitrogen uptake needs of plants, which makes perfect sense since the two cycles evolved with an interdependence on each other. The best of "time-released" chemical fertilizers can only attempt to copy the natural cycling of organic nitrogen. Any sort of large-scale sustainable agriculture would depend on first rebuilding soil organic matter nationwide. The vast majority of potentially available organic matter and nitrogen can be found in our municipal wastes and sewage. Large-scale composting of these materials could enable the rebuilding of the otherwise non-renewable soil organic matter on a national level, without which any large-scale departure from our current Monsanto-based, chemical, agro-industry isn't even remotely possible.

This was the first time I'd ever felt that I was working on something so important and worthy. I finally felt that I'd found the way I was supposed to contribute and enter a beneficial reciprocity with the earth. Compost still seems to me to be the most critical part of our foundation for the future, the substrate supporting the beginning and the end of the food chain.

As soon as I could afford to, I quit my construction job and began a private composting operation. I named our business Cacaloco Compost ("crazy shit" in Spanish). The name and the logo, "When it comes to compost, we're #1 and #2," proved good advertising and sales took off. I soon expanded from a small, illegal lot accepting horse bedding from all the wealthy, local equestrian facilities, back to a full-scale, permitted biosolids facility at a local landfill owned by Glenwood Springs.

The Glenwood Springs Landfill manager had fallen out of compliance with the state health department with some sub-standard sewage lagoons. Familiar with my experience in composting, the landfill manager offered me the lagoons and a large percentage of the revenues for sewage in exchange for bringing his operation into compliance. By that time, the permitting process had become so complicated and involved so many federal, state, and local agencies that I named my compost product "Bureaucrap."

With the Pitkin County compost facility struggling, I rapidly took over the biosolids and organic waste stream throughout our local region and beyond. We used to joke that whenever anyone flushed a toilet in western Colorado, we got a piece of the action. It had become a very profitable operation with a waste diversion rate of over 30%, by far the best I'd ever heard of. We were back in the lead of the compost industry.

Once again, our success drew the attention of our local bureaucrats who noticed that my successful diversion for beneficial use, a primary goal for all land managers at that time, was also diverting about a third of their revenue. The city had seen how much could be made and assumed they could replicate my efforts, and they consequently chose not to renew my ten-year contract. I had to watch another successful operation fall apart and fail.

Once again, my critters became my primary escape from the frustrations of human society. Kathy and I spent much time riding the back country. I would occasionally ride through town and tie up at bars under the pretense of keeping the critters "spook proof" and accustomed to traffic, but mostly I was trying to counter the changing nature and gentrification of my western world.

Hitchin' Post

Over the years, my mules have been in many fine eating and drinking establishments. These have mostly been peaceful and enjoyable experiences with the worst consequence being that I might be asked to leave while my mules are invited to stay. The one time that attracted the most attention from law enforcement was one of the times we didn't even ride into the bar, but rather left my critters tied outside.

It was a nice spring afternoon and my good friend, Brian, and I decided it would be a good day to get my half-broke donkey, Jorgé, used to traffic and all the other sights and sounds of civilization. While Kathy accurately accuses me of riding through towns merely to show off, it also happens to be one of the best ways of "spook proofing" equines. This is especially true for asses who, being much less affected by selective breeding for submission and therefore retaining much stronger survival instincts, maintain a distrust for any manmade, unnatural-looking objects, including white lines, yellow lines, dotted lines, sidewalks, curbs, changes in pavement surfaces, excessively straight sign posts, power poles and other suspicious, upright structures, excessively straight shadows from such vertical structures, their own shadows against suspiciously flat surfaces, manhole covers, drainage grates, underground culverts (they apparently hear the hollow sound underfoot), and everything else that might not be commonly encountered in deserts and other natural settings. For this reason, the simplest crossing of an intersection (did I mention stop signs and traffic lights?) can be a very time-consuming challenge.

It's very useful, if not practically essential, to have a familiar and trusted equine guide to lead the newcomer through these terrifying situations. While almost any trusted "town habituated" horse, mule, or fellow donkey will suffice for this purpose, mules and asses tend to prefer white mares for "follow the leader."

For this several-mile ride to our favorite bar and barbeque joint—Smoke, in Basalt—we decided to ride bareback with me on my "green-broke" donkey, Jorgé, and Brian riding double with his ten-year-old son, Eli, on my much more trustworthy mule, Zebadiah. The trip to town proved uneventful and we were soon crossing the town park across the street from Smoke, looking for a place to tie up. While there was a corral-looking lodgepole rail around Smoke's beer garden, it was more decorative than structural, and I'd had more than one bad experience involving insufficiently trained animals tied to insufficiently strong structures, including another similar fence around the beer garden at the Ship of Fools in Carbondale.

There was also a friend's front porch near the Ship of Fools, part of which was last seen careening down Main Street behind one of my mules. And just a few weeks earlier, I'd tied Jorgé and Zeb to a wheel-mounted trash dumpster behind the Brewpub in Carbondale. By the time I got back out to the beer garden with my drink, they'd already dragged the dumpster out into the middle of the street. The only thing preventing a high-speed runaway, smashing countless parked cars, was their disagreement on which way to run, resulting in a fairly static game of tug o' war. I'd then moved them across the street to an elm tree in front of the Forest Service building, which they'd thoroughly girdled by the time we went home. I felt a little bad about that destruction but after all, elm trees are on the state noxious weed list.

At any rate, I was becoming more discriminating in my choice of hitching posts and opted against the beer garden fence or the freshly planted and delicious-looking maple trees in the park and chose instead to tie off to the stout-looking steel lamppost securely anchor-bolted to a concrete foundation next to the sidewalk.

I was barely into my second (or third?) gin and tonic when a fellow barfly came over to report that there was quite a commotion going on around my critters. Coming out the door, I couldn't help but notice the large crowd gathered around the lamppost that was swaying back and forth alarmingly.

Mules and donkeys are much more playful than most people realize, and Zeb and Jorgé are exceptionally so, often wrestling, rearing and striking to the point of sometimes ending up down on their knees, exhausted and still nipping and biting at each other. Their nip and tuck rearing game had got the lamppost swinging back and forth to the extreme that I feared for the lives of the gathered crowd and hurried over to calm things down. Having pushed my way through the crowd to untie Zeb, I was greeted by five law enforcement officers from four different jurisdictions: two Basalt police, one Eagle County sheriff, one Pitkin County sheriff, and one state trooper, most of whom looked somewhat put out.

The Eagle County sheriff approached me first, demanding in an angry way, "Are these your animals?"

"Yes, sir. Is there a problem here?"

He looked at me like I was crazy, and he didn't even know where to start. "Those animals were acting crazy and creating a very dangerous situation."

"Well, sir," I said, "they're pretty playful."

Now the sheriff looked at me like I really was crazy, but he was at a loss for what to say. Brian and Eli had caught up by now and stood next to me, either for moral support or maybe just to get a better view. Brian has a very disarming smile and an irrepressibly respectable appearance. While every bit as rowdy and derelict as me, he just looks like one of the good guys and thus avoids a lot of trouble, often for both of us. Standing next to young, and even more innocent-looking Eli, added an even greater air of respectability and helped greatly to de-escalate the sheriffs' desire for conflict. But even so, they weren't quite ready to give in.

"What about all this horse shit on the sidewalk?" one of the Basalt cops asked.

I looked down at the sidewalk and said, "I don't see any horse shit." I was just buzzed enough to smart off a little.

This guy also looked at me like I was crazy, then paused for a second and said, "Well, mule shit, donkey shit, whatever! It's all the same, and we treat it just like we do dog shit in the park."

"Well," I said. "I always clean up after my animals and was planning to do so, but if you really want to treat this like dog shit, you might consider getting some bigger doggy bags and a bigger receptacle."

The cop didn't see any humor in this and was about to say something, but the crowd was chuckling and he kept his mouth shut.

Emboldened, I decided to show off Zeb's best trick. "You want to see a real smart ass?" I asked.

The cop stepped back and actually put his hand on the revolver. I tossed my hat down on the ground and Zeb picked it up and gave it to me. The crowd was all very impressed, but the cop was not.

"You might think this is all funny, but you better watch yourself. I might add harassment to whatever other charges we file."

"What other charges?" I asked.

"Endangering the public, creating a nuisance, possible damage of public property." He waved his arm across the trampled turf toward the lamppost. "They almost pulled that thing over. Someone could have been seriously injured or killed."

"Now, hold on," I said. "Have you ever heard of a hitching post law?"

"A what?" he asked.

"A hitching post law," I repeated. "It's a generic expression for laws that have become obsolete but were never removed from the books and therefore remain enforceable. They're referred to as hitching post laws because that's the most common one to remain on the books."

The cop now glanced uncomfortably at Brian as if checking his reaction and then back at his fellow officer. "Well, we wouldn't know anything about that," he said, trying to dismiss the topic. But the others, including the crowd, were listening and obviously curious, so I continued.

"Hitching post laws required businesses to provide enough hitching rail space out front to accommodate as many horses as they could accommodate people inside."

Now, for whatever reason, they all looked at Brian, my respectable alter ego. Brian was Pitkin County's public works director. He went to a lot of interagency meetings and also suffered excessive exposure with the media, so they might have recognized him, but I suspect it had more to do with his deceptively trustworthy appearance. With all eyes on him, Brian felt obliged to respond.

"I've heard of hitching post laws, and I think he's right. That is what they call those obsolete laws because it's the most common example."

Now the more aggressive Basalt cop turned back to me.

"Are you telling me that Basalt still has a law requiring hitching posts?"

"I don't know for certain, but I'd guess Basalt to be more likely than most to still have that law on the books. I'm only saying that before you start writing citations, you might want to know for sure who's outside the law."

By now, the state trooper had already lost interest and left. The two sheriffs were off to the side chatting about the weather or something, and the other Basalt cop was writing a citation to a motorcycle rider who had stopped to check out the commotion and apparently caused a traffic jam. Some woman walked up and asked if I could do the hat trick again because she hadn't caught it on video the first time. The frustrated Basalt cop interrupted the woman to take charge of the situation again. He needed to maintain control.

"Well, you can't leave these animals here on city property, so you need to leave."

"We just ordered our supper," I said. "It's probably sitting there getting cold even now."

"That's not my problem," the cop snapped. "I'm telling you to get these animals off city property right now!"

I pointed across the street to a small enclosure for trash dumpsters next to the Alpine Bank parking lot. "Is that city property?" I asked.

"No," he said. "I believe that's Alpine Bank's property. I can't give you permission to leave them there either."

"I'm not asking for permission," I said. "I'm one of their valued customers. Just let me know if they want to press charges for trespassing."

As I went to untie Jorgé, the cop turned back toward his car, apparently ready to give up and be rid of the situation.

The woman approached me again. "Could you do that hat trick again before you leave?"

Rifle

Shortly after I lost the Glenwood Springs Facility, the City of Rifle contacted me, wanting me to build and operate a compost facility for their wastewater facility. Slow learner that I was in dealing with any sort of government agency, I jumped right back into the fray. This time, it only took me a year or so to get crosswise with the bureaucracy, which was time enough to lose about half a million dollars invested in the new facility. Worse than that, I lost the dream I'd been pursuing, and achieving, for most of my adult life. My career and most important personal cause had suddenly been taken away and put out of reach. There was no way for me to afford to pay my debt and start a new facility. Furthermore, I was tired of getting pushed around and forced out of successful operations only to watch them fall apart. I kept being made to suffer for merely pursuing an honorable and worthwhile goal.

Even if I'd had the money and the drive to pursue another site, composting regulations and enforcement had changed drastically since I'd started my first operation. The first two compost facilities I started had required minimum engineering. In both cases, I'd designed the facilities and completed the operations plans and all other paperwork on my own, requiring an engineer only to review and approve my plans. The last facility I built in Rifle had cost over $100,000 in engineering alone.

Compliance with regulations had also become far more difficult. It was getting to the point that it was necessary to have full-time engineers and attorneys to run compost facilities. The days of the small mom and pop operations were a thing of the past.

Loss of Dreams

At about the same time the whims of bureaucracy wiped out my career, I was losing a battle for my other most important personal cause: the protection of wildlife.

After the initial thrill of having landed in the stronghold of wealthy environmentalists in Aspen back in the mid-eighties, I'd begun the unwelcome indoctrination into the fine and fading line between environmental green and greed green. Downzoning and various mechanisms such as conservation easements and green spaces not only help protect wildlife and the environment but also, not incidentally, serve to protect and enhance local property values. Much more than I allowed myself to admit, the "environmental ethic" in the Aspen area was financially motivated. When it came down to a choice between recreation and the tourist trade versus wildlife and the environment, profitability always won out. And what's worse is that self-proclaimed environmentalists, especially wealthy and well-known ones, can get away with far more environmental devastation than could any large corporation, industry, or other acknowledged environmental enemy.

The situation I was battling near Aspen involved the use of an abandoned railroad for a bike trail. It was the sort of project anyone would normally support except that it went through a designated wildlife sanctuary, including federally protected wetlands, a state and federally protected great blue heron rookery (nesting area), and designated critical winter habitat for several species, including deer, elk, and bald eagles (still on the federally protected endangered species list at that time). One would have assumed that it wouldn't be even remotely possible in this day and age for any sort of entity to jeopardize such a wealth of endangered wildlife and critical habitats. Only the wealthy hiding behind reputations of environmental protectors could possibly have gotten away with destroying so rare an environmental community. The ultimate wolves in sheep's clothing.

Many of the proponents of this recreational trail had been among the "environmental warriors" opposing me in the early days of weed control. They'd eventually become allies in my recycling, composting, and other environmental endeavors. I was amazed at how easily all these protectors of rain forests and of endangered fish and frog species could rationalize such exploitation of our local treasures for the sake of recreation and tourism.

Local intergovernmental agencies led by reputed "environmentalists and wildlife advocates" managed to obtain a categorical exclusion to avoid any sort of environmental impact statement or other environmental protections. Categorical exclusions are only available for federal transportation projects that can be proven to have no possible environmental impacts and, more specifically, to pose no potential threat to wetlands or wildlife habitats. It would have been difficult to even imagine a less appropriate situation for the use of a categorical exclusion. I was very vocal in pointing out the outrageously obvious hypocrisy of all our local pseudo environmentalists and once again became the target of tremendous wrath and resentment.

The ranch I'd lived on while studying the antelope winter habitat outside Maybell, Colorado was owned by a sheep rancher who had just gotten out of prison for shooting bald eagles from a helicopter. The Sheep and Wool Growers Association had a full-time coyote hunter and a pilot hired to hunt and shoot coyotes from the air in a Piper Cub airplane. They were active in trapping and poison baits and offered a bounty on coyotes.

The Colorado State Extension Service held a meeting for the S+WGA to promote the use of a coyote bait designed to sterilize male coyotes rather than poisoning them, so that coyote populations could be kept in check without the environmentally unpopular poisoning, shooting, and trapping. During the presentation, one of the old ranchers interrupted to say, "Son, I don't think you understand our problems out here. Them coyotes is eatin' our sheep, not fuckin' em."

Anyway, the ranchers' constant battle against wildlife was one of the issues that disillusioned me about the study I'd been conducting, resulting in my move to Aspen. The actions of those sheep ranchers against wildlife were exactly the sort of issues the Aspen "environmentalists" loved to criticize and attack. They were very active against obvious environmental enemies and distant offenses that don't require any personal sacrifice or compromise. They were fearless warriors when it was popular and easy. In reality, those Aspen types of fair-weather environmentalists can be far more dangerous than any number of outright coyote and even eagle killers. I'll take an honest enemy over an insidious chameleon any day. Give me the rancher with the rifle.

Once again, my mules provided me my best escape from life's frustrations. Hanging out with my chickens has always worked to relieve stress, but hanging out with my mules has done the most to help me make sense of things. Critters have always been important to me in working through emotions and finding purpose in life. They all seem to offer their own unique gifts.

The True Value of Critters

One of my best friends is almost ten times my weight. I'm glad he likes me. Other good friends aren't even a hundredth my weight.

The value of animals was first measured in the harvest of meat and hides. This eventually evolved into the use of hair and silk for fiber, and then the less destructive harvest of eggs, milk, and even blood for some African tribes and ancient Mongols, who regularly bled animals for this purpose. And don't forget the cliff swiftlet saliva for bird's nest soup. As the old saying goes, we've pretty much "used every bit of the hog except the squeal." And technically, we've even used the squeal to call in semi-feral hogs, which has evolved into a competition of sorts. (How do you spell soooooeeeeeyy!?)

Several species have been employed as a labor force in many various occupations and to increase our speed and mobility, probably initially for hunting and combat, but since evolving into many other practical uses and sports. One could continue indefinitely along these lines, but these are not the "true values" to which I refer.

Many of us find the company of animals to be more comfortable than that of other humans. The warm and fuzzy feelings of comfort and security provided by dogs probably have very deep roots in early society. While sporting proportionally larger brains, humans have always had weaker senses than most other animals and likely developed symbiotic relationships with various wild creatures long before any sort of domestication. Being tuned in to certain birds and mammals would provide early warning systems for the approach of large predators and/or the presence of potential prey. Ravens and wolves have long been associated with early humans and are likely candidates for this sort of symbiotic relationship. Such critters served as an extension of our own weak sensory system, improving our ability to survive. With domestication, these benefits were further strengthened. So, it's more than merely a warm and fuzzy feeling provided by critters. They actually provide significant security and good reason to feel more relaxed and comfortable.

Animals have always taught me far more, at least in the more important aspects of life, than people have. This is especially true in learning about other people and myself, largely because many animals share various actions, emotions, and expressions with people, without so great a tendency to hide their outward expressions or even use them to be deceptive, as we humans learn to do so early in life. That's not to say that animals aren't capable of deception. Some, such as ravens, are probably more adept along these lines than we humans are. But a basic and common example would be that of the old dog barking and pretending to detect an intruder to lead the young dogs in pursuit of spooks while it eats all the food.

Animal behaviorists warn against anthropomorphisms, the tendency to impose human characteristics on animals. And granted, I wouldn't assume a coiled snake to be happy to see me just because its mouth turns up at the corners like a strange smile. But some similarities are so obvious that it would be an exercise in idiocy to ignore them. In addition to helping us learn to read and interpret other humans and their intentions, animals demonstrate many important ideals and philosophies.

Going back to dogs as familiar examples, they teach us first and foremost about unconditional love and loyalty. Beyond that, they have infinite combinations of personalities. I've heard Jack Russells, one of whom I lived with for a quarter of my life, aptly described as "little criminals in clown suits," which certainly describes part of their dynamic personalities, although they're better known for bravery beyond their extensive brains. It's all been said about dogs: the bumper sticker, "I wish I was the person my dog thinks I am," Billy Currington's country western song, "Why caint you love me like my dawg does?" So, allow me to end this well-worn topic of dog traits by proclaiming without shame that I wish I were even half the man my old dog, Bo, was.

Animals specialize in the various lessons they provide. Horses teach us about spirit and free will. The moment a person sits on a horse, even a tame one that needn't be restrained to accomplish this, the horse moves differently, turning awkwardly on front legs instead of spinning gracefully on hind legs. The best-trained horse is one that moves as it would in the wild, except expressing the will of the rider, without knowing it's not making its own choices. Every time a horse, or any animal, is restricted in any way, as is often necessary in training, its free will, or spirit, is being chipped away, and it loses a bit of its most powerful inner strength. The best horse will never realize it has any limitations.

The early colonists in Africa attempted to train zebras to pull stagecoaches and perform other labor because domestic equines couldn't survive the tsetse fly. They soon learned that zebras have such a wild spirit that any efforts to confine and train them resulted in significant loss of strength and endurance, and eventually even the will to live. Zebras and their equine hybrids, zonkies (a cross between a zebra and a donkey) and zorses (a cross between a zebra and a horse), remain some of the most difficult to train. These lessons might be most applicable in raising children, whose wild and free spirits we always seem to battle when we should be trying to cultivate them.

Similar to horses, but different, are asses and mules. Mules are some of the most misunderstood targets of domestication. Probably everything you've heard about them is wrong. They're not stubborn, but patient and thoughtful, and they often have an opinion worth paying attention to. They're known for being steady, sure-footed, and reputed to be able to sense potential dangers undetected by others, which is why they're preferred in the most dangerous situations, such as traveling the Grand Canyon. They will not fall nor spook off a cliff.

Mules teach us about the importance of friendship, cooperation, and diplomacy in management practices. They are best "managed" as part of a cooperative partnership involving lots of gentle patience. They will not tolerate nor forget any abuse. Mules eliminate any possibility of Machiavellian management myths, especially along the lines of "it is good to be loved by your subjects, but necessary to be feared." Mutual respect is important, but if your mule fears you, you best get rid of it, or you will be hurt. Fear is never a good tool for interaction (except maybe when used for cheap thrills). One should fear anything that fears them. Fear is the most powerful and unpredictable of all emotions and is always dangerous.

Beyond direct lessons and philosophies, there are animals that specialize in various energy fields. Chickens, for example, are very proficient worriers. While some folks are aware of this trait (Chicken Little and the Sky is Falling), few (possibly only I) realize that they worry so efficiently and so much that they create an anxiety "sink." This excess of anxiety is so strong that they absorb the anxiety of any stressed out individual within the perimeter of their anxiety sink. (The perimeter area varies according to breed and environmental stress factors, according to my own extensive research.) So, if you have enough chickens and spend enough time with them, you will never need to worry again. And on a slightly more tangible level, chicken owners are always at least one egg breakfast and chicken dinner away from total destitution, and so really do have less to worry about. For those of you who find this narrative to be totally crazy, let me close in saying that, having plenty of chickens, I couldn't care less.

***

"Ownership" of critters, if you can call it that, can also be quite a responsibility. In many ways, we are "owned" by them. While Kathy and I love to travel, pets become a major limiting factor in our freedom to leave. Mules and horses aren't as much a problem in finding someone to feed them in our absence, but our dogs are even more part of our daily routine and are far more sensitive to our absences. They're used to spending much time outdoors and generally cover several miles a day with us. Thusly indulged (spoiled?), they would suffer terribly and possibly not even survive being kenneled with a stranger.

The last time we tried to board a dog, the owner of the kennel, a good friend of ours, called to report that our dog was refusing to eat or drink and wasn't pooping despite all their efforts to comfort and indulge her. We had to come home early. Fortunately, living here in the Southwest surrounded by unlimited and beautiful public lands, we have endless travel and adventure opportunities that include all our critters, right out our back door.

Mules and other equines involve a very long-term commitment. Horses can live over forty year and donkeys over sixty. Mules are somewhere in between. For us, animals are generally a life-long commitment. While most folks buy, sell, and trade equines on a regular basis, and there's certainly nothing wrong with that, the best relationship with critters is possible only when they're secure in the permanence of your relationship. Most animals, and certainly equines, are subject to emotions and psychological factors, especially along the lines of "abandonment fears." Sure, they can become accustomed to being passed around from owner to owner, but they do so the same way a human would—by learning not to get too attached.

For many of us, it's common to worry about our pets even more than we would our own kids. Much of this is due to the pets' inability to communicate their needs and their total dependence on us for so much. It's common for folks to grieve more over a pet's death than that of a close relative. Some folks go to extremes to keep pets alive long after they cease to enjoy life or suffer unreasonable pain. I've been guilty of that too many times and struggle to keep things in perspective. Spending thousands on a surgery for a fifteen-year-old dog strikes me as socially irresponsible considering how many hungry children might benefit from that investment. I've had to face similar battles of conscience.

When my mule, Zeb, was still young but already a very close friend and companion, he developed a serious case of colic, basically a potentially lethal belly ache caused by a blocked or twisted gut or excessive gas which, due to the equine inability to burb or regurgitate, can be very serious. As it became more prolonged and serious, the vet informed me that if he didn't start coming around within a few hours, the only option would be a surgery costing six to eight thousand dollars, with only about a 50% success rate. I initially stuck to my guns, believing it irresponsible, even to my own children's financial security, to spend that much on a long shot.

As the moment of truth approached, it occurred to me that I'd been on the verge of buying a new truck that would cost me well over $30,000. Suddenly, the choice became crystal clear. I would rather have Zeb than ten new trucks and would gladly never have another truck for the rest of my life if I could save him. I called the vet in a panic to let him know that I would spend any amount necessary to try to help Zeb. Much to my relief, he informed me that Zeb had started passing gas and pooping and seemed to be recovering. My conscience rested easy.

While asses and mules are reputed to be less prone to colic than horses, we've had more than our share of colic problems. About ten years after Zeb's struggle with colic, I came home to find Sexy rolling about in a colicky fashion. After walking her for hours, she finally farted and pooped a little, generally a sign of recovery, so I put her back out to pasture. Checking on her later that evening, I found her rolling again and appearing to be in pain. We took her to the vet and opted for the surgery they suggested, but we lost her anyway. I've always felt guilty for not having called the vet sooner.

It's a terrible feeling to think you might have caused injury to or jeopardized the safety of an innocent creature that depends upon and trusts you.

Being Worthy of Bo

While this book is mainly about my mules and donkeys, I feel I have to stop here and say something about my dogs, and one dog in particular.

Claiming to wish you were even half the man your dog was must sound rather self-deprecating to most folks. Not so to those who have known a dog like Bo the way I did. Bodiddly, as my then ten-year-old daughter had named him, was a dog of unknown breeding that looked more than anything like a slender, solid black golden retriever. He was indeed an outstanding, soft-mouthed retriever. He held an excellent point, flushed on command, and had all the qualities of a good bird dog. But he also seemed to have the herding instincts of a border collie and the qualities of both a guard dog and an emotional support pet at the same time. He was the most courageous warrior I've ever known and the kindest, gentlest caretaker you could ever hope to meet.

I could write an entire book about Bo's intelligence and heroism, but I'll try to demonstrate these qualities with two brief stories:

One evening as Kathy was taking our dogs for an evening stroll, our two small dogs, Paco and Otto, a miniature Australian shepherd and a short-legged Jack Russell, ran out ahead while Bo heeled close to Kathy. Up ahead, a pack of coyotes converged and attacked the two small dogs, having them down in seconds. Just as quickly,

Bo was in the midst of the battle and, although outsized and outnumbered, he overpowered and chased off the coyotes. In shock and seriously injured, Paco and Otto wouldn't have lasted another second. They'd suffered broken ribs and internal injuries, and Paco had required surgery on his herniated intestine, but they both ultimately recovered—thanks to Bo.

Another time, when I was raising a new flock of pullets (laying hen chicks), I'd started letting them out during the day and closing them back up in the coop with a heat lamp at night. When I went to bed that night, Bo came over to my bedside, obviously distraught and trying to lead me to the door. Having learned that he didn't behave this way without reason, I let him lead me out to the chicken coop, assuming something like a mink had gotten inside where he couldn't get to it. But instead of going to the coop, he went over to a willow thicket near the coop and started poking his nose in the tall grass and brush. I shone my flashlight around the thicket, thinking he was trying to show me some hidden predator, but I couldn't see anything. Just as I was prepared to leave, I heard the alarmed chirping of a chick. Bo became more agitated and finally reached into the tall grass, gently lifted out a small pullet, and set it at my feet. The chick had failed to follow the flock in that evening and Bo was smart enough to know that the bird shouldn't be left out.

Bo allowed us to keep bees, raise chickens, and maintain a productive garden and fruit orchard in a region that was otherwise ruled by wildlife, where bears would have destroyed fruit trees and beehives while deer grubbed off our garden and coons, coyotes, bobcats, and mink would have feasted on our chickens and eggs. He was a fierce protector of our property but never chased wildlife beyond our boundaries or when we were out in the wilderness. I always felt safe and secure with Bo at my side, whether I was in mountain lion country or a dark alley in a Mexican village. Neither man nor beast could ever approach me by surprise or do me harm without getting past Bo.

I've had many exceptional dogs, but Bo was an exception among exceptions. My current dog, Charro, is also so exceptional that I feel guilty for going on about Bo. A cross between a border collie and a blue heeler, he is every bit as smart as would be expected from these bloodlines and, like Bo, always seems to know what's going on and stays a step ahead of everyone. I don't recall ever having to train either of them even as far as housebreaking. Some critters naturally seem to know what they're supposed to do in any given situation.

Folks have always been impressed by my critters, even more so with dogs than with mules, and often ask me to help train their own dogs or mules. And while I have occasionally helped elderly or otherwise physically limited friends get a mule started under saddle, I generally turn down such requests because I truly am not a good trainer. What I do seem to be good at is establishing a trusting and respectful relationship conducive to mutual cooperation, which basically allows an animal to train itself. This isn't something I could instill in an animal in any number of training sessions or workouts. It's something that grows between us as we get to know each other and learn from each other.

It's difficult to explain, but my method of training is basically a holistic combination of trust, respect, love, and faith in each other, as though the desired outcome can be manifested or instilled in one another. A dog like Bo makes a person want to be worthy of him. He inspired me to try to be a better person. I believe this inspiration works both ways and most animals, when treated properly, will want to try to do better and please their human partners. Fortunately (and unfortunately), they seem to be better at that than we are. Most of my four-legged friends have been more than worthy of me, but I'm not sure I've ever really been worthy of them.

Needle in a Hayburner

All novice equestrians are coached to remain calm and try not to show any sign of fear or anxiety because horses are prone to pick up on such emotions and become more nervous and spookier themselves. While this information rarely helps to relax a beginner rider, and indeed usually has the opposite effect, it's still very useful knowledge to have when dealing with horses and more so with mules, who tend to be even more sensitive to their handlers' feelings. A handler being in a hurry is usually interpreted by mules as a problem of some sort that they might not want to be involved with.

My mules are some of the best and most cooperative I've ever known. They all come when called, stand for haltering, and can't wait to jump into a horse trailer. I won't own a problematic animal or even allow one in a pasture with mine. Problems such as being difficult to catch or difficult to keep fenced in seem to be very contagious. My mules like to go out riding and they cooperate in every way to help make this happen. Some will even start picking up halters off the ground and basically "ask"' to come along. My mule, Zeb, likes me and trusts me about as much as is possible for a mule.

Inspired by the lovable character Deets, from my all-time favorite western novel, *Lonesome Dove*, I decided I should always have a sewing needle handy. The freed slave,

Deets, always carried a large needle tucked into his pants for the constant repair required by his worn-out pants and for the occasional surgical needs that arise when one keeps the company of Texas Rangers. He probably saved Ranger Jake's life by digging out a mesquite thorn from the delirious Jake's swollen thumb, resulting from the mesquite thorn's poison. I rarely wear work gloves and so am constantly looking for needles to dig slivers and thorns out of my hands. This, along with the potential that I may someday need to sew something, prompted me to start carrying a needle. Not trusting my luck with a needle poking anywhere through my jeans, I opted to stash it in my hat band instead.

One morning, after having dug a few cactus spines out of the palm of my hand from a bad landing off a mountain bike, I went out to pet my mules. As they approached, I threw my hat out onto the ground, spinning it to make it land upright so Zeb could pick it up by the crown instead of crimping the brim and slathering the inside with saliva. Zeb bent down to pick it up as usual, but stopped mid motion and started sniffing around the brim. He apparently smelled the slight traces of my blood, or maybe traces of the infection from the festered cactus spines, on the needle stuck in my hatband. With an unbelievable dexterity of his lips rivaling that of a surgeon's fingers, he carefully plucked the tiny needle from my hat band, and I watched in horror as it disappeared into his mouth.

Now, had it been a cow swallowing that needle, I wouldn't have given two hoots. Not only have I never been so attached to a cow as I am to Zeb, but the needle probably wouldn't have posed much threat to a cow. I've seen ranchers and even veterinarians poke unsterile pocketknives into the bloated gut of a cow to release the gas, without causing infection and with full recovery. Such a poke would be a death sentence to an equine. They are far more prone to systemic infections in their digestive tracts and might not survive the painful passage of a needle without expensive and doubtful surgery.

I had no lead rope nor even belt with me. I thought about taking off my shirt to put around his neck but decided that might be enough out of character to raise suspicion. If I did anything wrong right now, my best friend would likely jog away watching me over his shoulder as he swallowed the needle. The thought of that filled my head with an explosion of adrenaline as I tried to approach one of the world's best lie detectors acting as though I hadn't a worry in the world.

Typically, once I threw my hat out for him, I would generally ignore him, refusing to feed or pet him, until he retrieved my hat. So just approaching him like that was already a breach in protocol that could make him suspicious. Routine and protocol are very important to mules. Having been close friends with Zeb for almost fifteen years, since he was a baby, I still need to go through certain formalities with every fresh encounter. Even when he comes running to me, anxious to go for a ride, I still need to respect his space until invited into it. If I were to be in a hurry and try to just halter him right off the bat, he would likely step back and question my intentions. No, I must first hold my hand out to sniff as one might do with a stray dog, even though he obviously knows who I am or wouldn't have come running up in the first place. Once he reaffirms my odor, he will drop his head to have his ears scratched and then rise up to shake his head vigorously before wanting the halter put on.

I managed to keep my hands calm and confident as I let him sniff me and then scratched him along his muzzle just below his eyes as most mules like. He dropped his head for me to rub his ears as usual, which I did, but I kept a hand on his muzzle when he rose up again to keep him from shaking his head as he normally would in response to ear scratching. I didn't want to lose track of the needle during his shaking action. If I lost the needle, I would have to proceed as if he'd swallowed it, including a trip to the vet, doubtful x-rays, endless worry and stress. I continued rubbing his muzzle as I started working the fingers of my other hand into the corner of his mouth. As I gripped my hand around his limp, sponge-like tongue, I knew this was the moment of truth.

Equines have various vulnerable spots that allow a handler to immobilize large animals with minimum effort. Young horses can often be frozen in place by flexing their tail up over their back—but not always. A little more effective, but almost sure to make a horse head shy, is twisting down an ear. A good bite on the upper lip will immobilize almost any horse, mule, or donkey and, although I've been guilty of hanging off a horse's lip like a bulldog, most folks use a pinching tool called a "twitch" for this. Pulling a horse's tongue out to the side and hanging on is supposed to be another immobilization technique that I'd seen before but had never tried. Zeb had always been such a good boy that he'd never had to experience any sort of efforts to restrain him, and I was afraid that any such effort now might be sufficiently alien as to make him panic. I managed to get a hold of his tongue without any abrupt or spooky movements and hang onto it as calmly as I could, trying to make this strange behavior seem as routine as possible.

He pulled back, stretching out his tongue with its weird feeling of soft, rubbery flesh and very weak muscles, but he did so slowly and carefully as I continued petting and reassuring him with my other hand and with my voice as I choked back my own panic. He was starting to relax back toward me when I saw the needle on the side of his tongue just about to disappear back into his mouth. I managed to pull just hard enough to keep his tongue out without causing him to sit back again and smoothly slid my free hand across his muzzle to retrieve the needle. Zeb continued standing there, looking somewhat puzzled and curious, as I stood staring at the needle and feeling the relief wash away the adrenaline. I was literally weak in the knees—exhausted by the weight of the tiny needle I held so tightly between my thumb and forefinger.

Sanchez

It was hard to think about wanting another animal after Sexy's heartbreaking death, and I wasn't really looking for one. It seems that critters generally do a pretty good job of finding me. While bullshitting at a bar, an outfitter friend of mine joked that he had the perfect mule for me.

Naturally, I was curious about what could be so wrong with the mule that my friend wanted to palm him off on me. Turns out he was a bit of an attack mule. Not totally random attacks; he appeared to have something against four-wheelers. One of the "wranglers" was trying to herd horses into the corral, chasing them with a four-wheeler, and the mule charged and jerked the kid off the 4x4 by the scruff of his coat.

I thought that was great! I've never liked those four-wheelers and really hate seeing anyone chasing horses or livestock on one, so I didn't see any problem with a mule like that. He was young, trim, athletic, and very likable. One quick ride and I was happy to give seven hundred for him. A very young mule, he had the personality of a goofy teenager—generally distracted, sometimes problematic, always lovable. He was almost too friendly, to the point of being uninhibited and even unintimidated by humans. I'd always thought such traits to be desirable in critters, but a total lack of intimidation can lead to a lack of respect. He was so friendly that I was really surprised when he laid his ears back and charged me one morning while I was bent over climbing through a fence. I was quick enough to straighten up and wave him off before he closed in, but he'd looked serious and dangerous. Messing around with him over the next few days, I discovered that he was most triggered by dark, puffy coats, when a person was on all fours or hunched over in a similar position.

I talked with a couple wranglers who had worked with Sanchez in the past. They confirmed that it was more than just ATVs, and that he did seem triggered by dark clothing and bending over. I also discovered that Sanchez had been bottle fed due to his mother's death. There seems to be some sort of syndrome associated with bottle fed equines. I've come to believe that bottle feeding, and thus replacing the mother, puts the human on an equal basis with the foal, leading to the lack of respect.

While it's great to be accepted as "part of the herd," it isn't safe to be treated as such. Equines play much rougher with each other than they do with humans. Mothers (and bottle feeders?) are subject to the pecking order and are thus fair game for aggression. A similar attack by Sanchez on another horse wouldn't seem unusual. Sanchez's problem amounted to a failure to distinguish between two- and four-legged critters. There's a documentary on a horse trainer named Buck Brannaman. He encounters a young stud horse that had been bottle fed and was occasionally triggered into violent attacks similar to those witnessed with Sanchez.

I liked everything else about Sanchez, so I worked diligently to try to resolve his issues, approaching him repeatedly bent over in a dark coat and then, as gently as possible, waving him off and trying to comfort and calm him at the same time. I finally thought I really had him through it and continued daily to try to trigger him without reaction. Then one day, Kathy was wearing a dark coat and bent over to lift up a toppled hay feeder, and Sanchez snapped again and attacked her, biting her hard enough to draw blood even through her Carhartt coat. I thank our lucky stars that he only bit and didn't strike Kathy, and that Kathy was quick enough to scoot out under the fence before he did more serious damage.

I shudder to think of what could have happened if one of my girls or some other neighbor kid had gone into that pen, and I knew Sanchez should be put down. But I'd also become very attached to him and couldn't bring myself to do it. I called the outfitter who had sold him to me and told him that I was ready to take the loss and didn't want my money back, but that he had to come get the mule and put him down. He came and got him but never put him down. I still feel bad about that and am still angry with the outfitter and with myself. I sure hope that Sanchez never really hurt anyone… or at least not anyone who didn't deserve it.

Back to Texas

As far as my own health and well-being went, I was broke, in huge debt, unemployed, and dis-spirited. In our situation, the only reasonable solution was bankruptcy, but we'd lived in the valley for thirty years and knew everyone, and we felt that our reputations were our most valuable assets. Only the bank would have taken a loss, but we knew all the bankers, too, and we felt tight-knit with the entire community. Kathy went to work in property management for someone she could barely tolerate while I continued working the small, illegal horse bedding compost operation that I'd kept going over the last dozen years.

When the site for that operation sold and I lost even that small bit of employment, I started working construction and various odd jobs around the valley. At this point, I entered an all-time low in my wild ups and downs. Losing my career and personal cause to government regulations was disappointing but shouldn't have come as any great surprise. And alienating the pseudo-environmental crowd in Aspen was no big deal. I'd grown accustomed to the fair-weather participants in life. But losing some of the best wildlife habitat I'd ever known, right in my backyard, was devastating. I felt discouraged, defeated, and lost. When my sister, Peg, called to ask if I might help out at the ranch, I jumped at the opportunity to spend time at one of my favorite stomping grounds of my youth.

Peg's husband, John, had passed away the previous year, and she'd handed the ranch property down to her daughters. With the cattle gone and less human presence on the place, they were having increasing problems with trespassing and poachers. The fences were in disrepair and the area was becoming more populated as surrounding ranches sold and subdivided. They were also having trouble with an invasive species of eastern red cedar that had taken over during a several decade drought and was crowding out the more desirable loblolly pine and live oak plant communities.

While undesirable for its ability to suck moisture, acidify soil, and crowd out other vegetation, eastern red cedar is the tall, straight variety of cedar very resistant to decomposition and desirable for fence posts. I packed up my chainsaw and fencing tools and headed south.

Cedar Chopper

"That your trailer load of cedar out there?" Hauling a load of cedar turned out to be a sure-fire conversation starter.

"Yessir, it is." Everyone called me "sir" down there in Texas. I've never felt like a sir and so have never been fond of this courtesy. Tired of explaining that I wasn't a sir, I'd learned to preempt others and simply out sir them. There seemed to be room for only one sir in most conversations.

"Good looking load of cedar."

"Thank you, sir."

"You a cedar chopper?"

"Well, sir, I use a chain saw. Does that still count as a chopper?"

He looked at me like I was crazy. "They all do."

That hadn't been the case when I was in this area forty years ago. Cedar choppers all used axes back then and were a pretty scary crowd—the sort we told horror stories about around campfires as children. They were actually scornful about the use of chainsaws and considered anyone using one to be the ultimate pussy. Most were missing at least one finger and, to those brave enough to talk to them, always had a story about being snake bit on the finger far from any medical care and choosing to just chop it off so they could get back to work.

As a young, long-haired cowboy, I'd been warned against dealing with them. "Don't never mess with them fellers," Kyzar had told me, "unless you're ready to kill or die." Even the other rednecks avoided eye contact with them in a bar. Their axes were never far away. Kyzar had told me a story about one of them impaling another chopper's head to the floor of the dance hall during a Bob Wills show out in West Texas. They'd just roped off that section of the dance hall and continued the music. The closest law was hours away, there was no phone, and this was, after all, Bob Wills. Who would ever miss Bob Wills over just one more dead cedar chopper?

Now I was one of them.

Kyzar was a disheveled and dumpy West Texas cowboy who looked and sounded like an uneducated backwoods hick. In reality, he'd graduated top of his class at Texas A+M School of Veterinary Medicine and was one of the smartest people I'd ever met. He had been a partner in my brother-in-law, John's, large animal veterinary practice, and I had often accompanied him on large animal calls. He became my first real mentor and role model, although he would never consider himself to be either.

"You a Stark?" The same old gentleman startled me back to the present time on the front deck of the Roadhouse Restaurant outside Paige, Texas. The question caught me off guard. The Starks had been the paternal side of my family several generations ago, and my great-great- (great?)- granddaddy had founded the town of Starkville, South Dakota, eventually renamed Unityville, and now a ghost town. This was more than I felt like explaining.

"No sir, I'm a Duke. But I have some cousins named Stark up north. Why? Who are they?"

"They're cedar choppers over there to the Smithville area."

"Well, sir, good chance we're related, but I don't think I'll go out of my way to meet them. Haven't met too many cousins I care for or am proud of." I didn't include that I was thinking of David Duke, head of the KKK, and hoping he wasn't a relative. This guy was probably a fan of his. Anyhow, that statement seemed to close the conversation for the time being.

I was camping and cutting cedar on a small ranch owned by some of my extended family west of Paige on Paint Creek Road. I'd lived here while attending the University of Texas in Austin part time and helping my brother-in-law run this ranch the rest of the time. Apparently, these cedar were a fast-growing, invasive species that had taken over much woodland during the several decade long drought Texas had suffered in my absence.

My nieces, who had asked me for some help with their fences, were also trying to cut back the cedar invasion. They hadn't had much luck hiring local cedar choppers and asked if I might be interested. I'd built a couple log cabins and have always wanted to build one out of cedar. I figured I could make a little money hauling fence posts back to Colorado, and eventually haul back enough logs to build a small cabin. Not ready for retirement, but basically unemployable, I had plenty of free time and couldn't pass up hanging out on my old stompin' grounds. I looked forward to some bass fishing, hog hunting, and just hanging out in the woods, so I decided to do some cutting.

There were a lot of large cedar trees, so I started hauling logs to sell to a local sawmill. I found myself basking in the praise of my "nice load of cedar" and started feeling an unreasonable pride in being a lowly cedar chopper, sometimes making unnecessary stops at gas stations, quick marts, bars, or whatever on my way to the sawmill just to increase the chances for compliments on my load.

One morning as I fueled up, a wild-eyed old trucker came hobbling over to check out my load. Hardly glancing at the load, he held eye contact for an uncomfortably long time before saying through a nearly toothless grin, "You got it, ain'tcha?" I assumed he was saying I "had it together" or "got it right" or was in some way complimenting my load, so I responded by agreeing that it was a nice load. He just kept staring and grinning, not really listening as much as reading me. "My daddy told me that once ya git that cedar sap on yer hands, ya cain't never get it off."

I found his laughing eyes and knowing grin to be more than a little invasive—kind of like being teased by Rumpelstiltskin. I replied, "Yeah, well, it is hard to wash off."

He was obviously just watching and not listening. "Yup, ya got it awright." He grinned as he released me from his stare and turned back toward his truck, chuckling all the way.

Something about him was a little unnerving and I was glad to see him go, although I knew he hadn't entirely left me.

Texas was suffering a record hot May that year and by late in the month, the temperatures were in the nineties every day with nearly 100% humidity. I was getting tired of being stung by fire ants and always watching out for copperheads, water moccasins, rattlers, scorpions... You name it. Just dropping big cedar trees was dangerous enough by itself without all the other hazards. They had lots of big branches hiding the trunk and skewing the weight such that it was very difficult to judge which direction they wanted to fall.

To make it worse, the ground cover was thick with post oak, yaupons, and many other shrubs that could snag clothing like so many fishhooks, not to mention all the poison ivy and the appropriately named bastard vine (nature's prototype for barbed wire) making escape routes difficult. It's hard to walk any distance through these woods without drawing blood. With trees falling the wrong way and catapulting unseen deadfalls through the air, attached to the canopy by a network of vines, I had close calls every day.

Just operating a chainsaw is sufficiently dangerous that it shouldn't be done alone, much less miles from other people. While I carried a cell phone in case of emergencies, it wasn't hard to visualize a thousand different scenarios where I would be unable to access it. Even if someone was checking on me, they would have a hard time finding me in several hundred acres of thick woods if I were unconscious. If it was more than a day or two, my place of death would probably be discovered by the presence of my chainsaw and maybe my boots and odd shreds of clothing because by then, my fleshless bones would have been well scattered by wild hogs. Sounds pretty dark and gruesome, but not far from reality. I was starting to wonder if I had some sort of death wish. It was beginning to feel like a compulsion.

It reminded me of a mentality I'd witnessed in some old mining towns around Colorado. There's a weird sort of addictive attraction to extracting something valuable from the earth that has persisted many years after the gold rush. It's somehow more involved than just the notion of getting something for nothing. While the attraction of striking it rich is understandable, this same mentality keeps coal miners motivated to work underground in spite of all the hazards and health risks. That hardly seems like something for nothing.

I tried to compare my cedar compulsion to the pleasures derived from hunting and fishing, or even just gathering berries or mushrooms and such. I've always figured that the tremendous satisfaction generated by these activities had to do with an almost instinctive fulfillment of ancient activities stemming from a history as hunter/gatherers. But maybe it has more to do with the "something for nothing" mentality than I would like to admit. Could that be the driving force behind my unreasonable pursuit of "just a few more trees"? The hard work and adverse conditions could hardly be considered something for nothing. And there certainly wasn't any chance of striking it rich. Running a noisy chainsaw is hardly a fun and healthy nature experience like gathering berries. So, what was going on with me out here in the woods?

I'd already been down there longer than I'd planned, but I was making pretty good money hauling logs to the mill. There was something very attractive about the simple beauty of hard and dangerous work being rewarded with cash at the end of each day, followed by a couple cold Lone Star beers and a burger at the Roadhouse in Paige. After checking my bedding for snakes and scorpions each night, exhausted sleep came easy, serenaded by cicadas, tree toads, and the mariachi calls of the barred owls. Plus, I'd already scoped out some easily accessible, big, beautiful trees that I felt compelled to harvest before I was done, and there was still the load I planned to haul back to Colorado to build my tiny, cedar log home. There was always one more tree a little deeper in the woods that I just couldn't resist going after.

"You got it, ain'tcha?" the old man's voice echoed in my head. *"Once ya git that sap on yer hands..."* I found myself rubbing the sandy soil through my fingers to remove the stickiness as I sat on a log to sharpen my saw. That old man didn't know shit! He probably didn't even know that these "cedars" weren't really even cedars, but junipers. He certainly didn't know anything about me! He couldn't look into my head and read my thoughts like some ugly little elf. I could leave any time I wanted, I thought as I squinted through the yaupons and scrub oaks, trying to relocate the big cedar that was to be my next target.

It wasn't quite nine A.M. and I was already drenched in sweat. Dirty rivulets of sweat stung the countless bug bites and bastard vine cuts that covered my arms and any other exposed flesh. A scorpion scrambled off as I re-positioned my saw to continue sharpening the chain. What was keeping me here? Why did I need that next tree—and the next one after that? It was time to go home. But I already knew I would be back, maybe when it cooled off a little this fall. Not so many snakes out during winter.

Shit! The sap is on me! The sap is in me! The sap is me!

Baby Acapulco's

The huge bass made one last spectacular leap before I finally landed him. At least five pounds, he would provide several meals. His battle had lasted until it was nearly dark and had pulled my leaky canoe back into a swampy little cove resembling a gator-infested Louisiana bayou, with vines and Spanish moss groping down from the dense canopy above. With my hands full fighting the big bass, I hadn't been able to bail the leaky canoe, and I debated whether I should take the time to bail water or take my chances on getting back to the clearing before I swamped. The banks of the cove were way too thick with thorny vegetation to land the canoe. While I knew he wasn't real, I could feel the presence of the "monster" and couldn't get the tipsy, water-logged boat back to the clearing fast enough.

My campsite on the farm had water piped to it, and the days were hot enough that the cold water felt good on all my bug bites and bastard vine cuts, and there were also several cow ponds close by that I used to swim in decades ago when I'd lived here. It had been a working ranch in those days, with over two hundred cow/calf pairs, and a dip in the closest pond at the end of a hot day had been a standard practice. But there's something about relaxing in hot water that just can't be replaced by any amount of cold water, and I'd somehow over the years become phobic about swimming in the ponds. It was probably just an increased awareness of water moccasins and snapping turtles, but it might have had to do with rumors started by one of my nieces.

There had been some sort of exotic animal farm in the neighborhood during my decades of absence, with rumors that many critters had escaped or been released upon the place closing down. My niece who spends the most time at the farm swears she saw either a giant python or anaconda swimming around one of the ponds on several occasions. Either a giant snake or some sort of Loch Ness monster, she wasn't exactly sure, other than that it was very large and swam holding its head two or three feet out of the water. When it submerged, it retracted backward like a snake recoiling instead of diving forward like a bird might do. Even though my sister (generally not nearly as bold as myself) still swims in these ponds, I've developed a bad case of the heebie jeebies and get nervous even paddling around in the leaky canoe.

In spite of bad dreams about huge snakes, there was something addictive about hanging out on the farm, hunting hogs and cutting cedar, or just wandering around in the woods. The bass fishing was better than ever although, even on dry land, I started getting a little anxious after dark. For whatever reason, I just couldn't get enough of hanging out on the farm all by myself. Friends and relatives in Austin, who were anxious to catch up after all these years, were puzzled and maybe even a little concerned about my reclusive ways. Probably the main thing was just being on my own schedule and not accountable to anyone else, but I was finally ready for a hot shower, a stiff drink, and some social time.

It was just a couple blocks to walk from my sister's house to Baby Acapulco's down on East Riverside. There were also a couple other good restaurants within easy walking range including an excellent taqueria, but I was interested in a purplerita, the signature Baby A's drink so strong that it was limited to two per customer. When my brother had ordered one the last time I was in town and bragged about how strong it was, I'd scolded him for drinking such a grotesque-looking and sounding drink just for a buzz. Now it was sounding pretty good. And Baby A's was the most likely place to have any sort of interesting social action.

When I walked through the door, the first thing I saw was two middle-aged and very conventional-looking men who apparently couldn't keep their hands off each other. While I have several gay friends and have always thought I was pretty open-minded and progressive about such things, I've never been favorably impressed by extreme forms of public displays of affection. Even so, this particular display struck me as somehow more offensive than most. It made me wonder if hanging out on the ranch was starting to affect me. Maybe I really was turning into one of those redneck old cedar choppers. I headed past them toward the bar, hoping to change my cranky attitude.

Once seated and trying to power down my gawdawful purplerita, I still couldn't help but notice these guys in my peripheral vision, or in the bar mirror, or just about anywhere I tried or tried not to look. They were by far the most animated and active people in the restaurant, holding and feeling and wringing each other's hands together. That's when I noticed the white cane propped against the wall behind one of them. I glanced over as surreptitiously as I could—

it wouldn't have mattered if I'd openly stared because they were so caught up with each other, signing into each other's hands, that they were totally oblivious to their surroundings and blind anyway. But wait a minute. Why would blind guys be signing to each other? Were they deaf and blind? No. Look again. That one guy had reading glasses perched up on his forehead. Was he deaf? Why else would they be signing? Or was his boyfriend blind and deaf? Why would I still assume this was his boyfriend? There was nothing sexual going on, just a very enthusiastic and intimate conversation. They were most likely just very good friends with a lot to catch up on and probably not many others they could communicate with.

I looked around the rest of the restaurant. There were several couples scattered around, one with two children. Everyone in the entire restaurant, except for these two men and a couple guys at the bar watching a football game on a TV in the corner, were pecking away at iPhones. None of these people, except for those two men, were in any way engaged with each other. I looked back at the two men without feeling any further need to be candid. No one would have noticed if I'd stripped naked and started doing back flips. I'd never witnessed such an intimate, animated, enthusiastic, and focused conversation in my whole life. At that moment, the apparently blind man had both hands on his friend's fist, which was enthusiastically nodding up and down in an obvious affirmative "cognate" that even I could understand. These men had made a gift of any "handicaps" involved, and I experienced a strong envy for their involvement with each other.

Why had my initial impression been so negative? While I've never been very religious, I've always found wisdom in the admonition "ours is not to judge" and have tried to incorporate and practice at least that much. Many of my regrets in life have involved pre-judging others. It's a trait hard to tolerate in others. How could I let such nonsense still guide my thoughts and feelings? I thought I'd learned this same lesson too many times and had finally taken it to heart. Apparently not.

Now I wanted to get to know these guys and learn their story. I wanted to be part of what they had going on. I thought about introducing myself and trying to compliment them in some way for... what? Having a conversation? Being interested and interesting? What could I say? "Didn't mean to eavesdrop, but..." Could you call it "eavesdropping" when nobody was speaking? I mean talking? Vocalizing? I really wanted to somehow let them know what a positive impact they'd imparted upon me but felt that any sort of interruption of their intense focus would be unwelcome. Then I realized the true cause of my reluctance: my own initial negative reaction and impression had made me unworthy of their company. I paid for my unfinished purplerita and headed back across the street for a taco. I'd had enough socializing and suddenly felt like I needed a little more time alone on the farm. Maybe I could make peace with the monster in the pond.

***

Having survived the jungles of the Yucatan, Kathy wasn't too excited about moving into a neighborhood of poisonous snakes and creepy crawlers, especially one that didn't even have a beach and ocean. While she enjoys hunting and fishing and enjoyed a few days at a time on the ranch, she's never been much impressed by Texas in general, so I eventually had to come back to Colorado. Not looking forward to the aimless pursuit of odd jobs and such, I was fortunate enough to be given yet another chance to relive my youth as a trail guide and to be able to once again work with my own critters.

Huntin' Guide

It all started, as have many aspects of my life, with some basic bar room BS. A wrangler friend came into a favorite bar sporting a fresh black eye. While this isn't an unusual situation for most young wranglers and cowboys, Chuck was in his early seventies and not the fighting type. I knew from personal experience that black eyes among us older folks tend to be more of a source of embarrassment than a badge of courage. I'd just the previous year been riding home from our local rodeo in Carbondale, Colorado on my adorable and friendly, but untrained, young jenny ass (burro).

Although I admit to having a few shots of whiskey and maybe a beer or two offered by well-meaning friends at the rodeo, this is hardly uncommon for most cowboys riding home from evening events and wasn't considered to be a factor in falling off my ass. It had more to do with being bareback on a pitch-black, moonless night along a heavily wooded stretch of a black asphalt bike trail when my little darlin', Lucky, happened to spook at an unseen monster in the brush. Due largely to the vertigo caused by the darkness (I'm certain), I didn't even realize I was falling, nor did I see the rapidly approaching asphalt, until I saw the brilliant flash of my face impacting the asphalt. I woke up already on my feet and trying to calm down my distraught donkey with the lead rope miraculously still in my grip.

At any rate, I was familiar with the embarrassment of a black eye on an older man. Everyone just assumes we fell down in the bathtub or something. But good cowpokes never allow a little empathy to interfere with some good razzing.

"Little old to be fightin', ain't ya, Chuck? Piss off some old widow woman or somethin'?"

"Naw, them old biddies in our dude string are starting to get a little cranky this time of year. I was trying to correct an old mare that was getting out of hand with our guests when she reared back and smacked me in the face with her head. Damnear fell off a dude horse! We've been havin' so many wrecks lately, we're about out of wranglers."

"Well, hell, I used to do a little dude wrangling. Let me know if y'all need some help." I'd assumed that to be the end of it. Just typical bar room banter… until about a week later when I got a call from Chuck's boss looking for a new wrangler. "Chuck gives you his highest recommendations," my future employer informed me. I found this curious, since Chuck and I had never seen each other riding anything four-legged other than bar stools. I couldn't help but ask, "Oh, yeah? What did he tell you about me?"

There was a considerable pause before Brian responded. "Well, he said you seem to be able to hold your tequila and that he's never seen you without your hat on."

"That's true," I said. "Sounds like pretty good qualifications for a cowboy to me." I'd recently committed to increasing my part-time commitment working with a friend and so told Brian that, as much as I appreciated the offer, I was tied up with other obligations. I was, after all, a darn near full-grown adult with serious commitments and obviously couldn't just drop other obligations to go play cowboy. Even as I explained all this to my new boss, my wiser subconscious was reminding me that I'd never regretted anything I'd done near as much as I'd regretted those things I hadn't done. It took me about thirty seconds to reconsider and call my friend to rearrange my schedule down to two days a week.

I then called Brian back and told him that if the position was still open, and if I could use my own mules, I would be there first thing in the morning. Thus began the most entertaining employment I'd had since the last time I'd been a trail guide over forty years earlier. It hardly felt like work, riding my mules through the beautiful Maroon Bells Wilderness Area, even though I had to worry about overweight and inexperienced riders falling off the poor horses that were cinched too tight to help prevent this. But other than tight saddles, which they were used to and toughened against, these horses were treated very lovingly and seemed to enjoy their work. This was due to the fact that a young woman, Meagan, was in charge of the operation instead of some mean old ex-bull rider or someone of that sort, so often in charge of dude horse operations.

As the season wound to a close, Brian informed me that his brother, Shawn, could use some help with his outfitting operation in the north part of the Flattops Wilderness area outside Meeker, Colorado. I happily accepted this offer on the same condition of using my own mules. Now, Shawn and Brian were excellent horsemen. They'd made their livings with horses for their whole lives. They were both accomplished trainers, farriers, owners of large strings of horses, and were very experienced packers and guides. Neither of them, however, was very keen on mules. Shawn seemed to be particularly predisposed against mules (not uncommon among horsemen who've had a bad mule experience), but he apparently really needed some extra help in a hunting camp and so accepted my conditions.

On my first day at work, the day before the first rifle season, I was showing some hunters how my mule, Zeb, would fetch my hat for me when I threw it out on the ground. Shawn happened to be walking by right about then and turned around to say, "Yeah, I know a guy with a mule that will lie down for him to get on, but it won't go within a hundred yards of a dead elk!"

This was my first inkling as to Shawn's prejudice against mules. "Don't worry, Shawn. My mules have packed many an elk."

Now he walked over to face me more directly. "Those mules don't even have any shoes on!" he asserted very forcefully.

"These mules have very tough hooves," I said. "They don't need shoes." Some of the traits I look for in mules are black and very upright, cupped hooves. Dark hooves tend to be harder than light colored or striped hooves. Flat, "pancake" hooves are far more prone to chipping and splitting.

"No hooves are harder than granite," he countered. "One trip to upper Paradise Lake and they'll be crippled for the rest of the season."

"Well, if that happens, I guess I'll have to ride a horse. You got anything short enough for an old fart like me to climb up on?" I teased.

That lightened it up enough to end on a good note. As he turned to walk away, he said, "Just be down here at 4:30 in the morning." Then he stopped and turned back as if to check me out a little closer. "Better make that 4:20."

I was down at the stables at 4:00 the next morning. Not knowing the country around there, I'd assumed I'd been hired as a wrangler to help gather and saddle horses and maybe pack gear and game when necessary. It hadn't even occurred to me that I might actually be guiding hunters. I'd hunted most of my life but had never guided other hunters. And I'd always been a meat hunter rather than a trophy hunter and favored cows over bulls, so I'd never spent much time learning to bugle bulls in or caping out a rack for mounting or other things a guide should know.

"Okay, now," Shawn said the next morning. "You're gonna have a pretty important client today. He's the Elk

Foundation guy that purchased this hunt through the Elk Foundation National Annual Dinner Banquet. We want him to be treated as a VIP with extra special attention."

He must have noticed my surprise because he turned and added, "Don't worry. I know you're not familiar with this area. I'll line you out on the way up in the truck."

I wondered why he would be putting the unknown new guy with a "pretty important client" and figured his brother, my previous boss, must have given him some kind of good recommendations. A few minutes later, Shawn returned and told me that I would have to drive a separate truck, but not to worry, he would fill me in with the day's plans at the trail head.

Unloading horses at the trail head, it became obvious that I was the only one around without a headlamp. I'd never owned a headlamp, preferring to stumble around in the dark, claiming that I was thusly enhancing my night vision. This wasn't a viable option when guiding city folk around in the dark, so I had to confess my lack of preparation and beg a loaner from Shawn. Another rung down the ladder of success.

"You got your radio, don't ya?" Shawn asked.

"Radio?" I'd always thought it was illegal to carry a radio while hunting.

"Well, I hope you at least grabbed your lunch," Shawn said as I walked back to get my mule. I pretended not to hear him and kept going. Having tried to be as helpful as possible during my first day of confusion about which horses and which saddles went with which hunters, I'd missed breakfast and didn't even have any water with me. I wasn't making much of an impression so far. I was the only one within miles not wearing at least a day pack. I'd always hunted from remote camps that provided hunting directly from camp. My style had always been going for a morning hunt, then returning to camp for lunch and maybe a nap before going out for the evening hunt. I'd developed the unhealthy habit of never getting thirsty and so rarely carried water.

After about an hour's ride to where we would be hunting, Shawn pulled me aside to direct me in my hunt in the pitch darkness of pre-dawn. Waving his arm toward the darkness, he told me there was a ridgeline behind us that I should follow up, staying as close as possible to the lip of the ridge over the creek (*what ridge? what creek? I couldn't see a thing!*). As I approached the top, he said, and this should be fairly obvious because the trees became thicker at that point, making travel more difficult (*what does that mean?*), I should be able to see an elk wallow down in the bottom off to my right.

With a plan as clear as mud, I headed out with my important hunter. A slight blizzard blew in and the already frigid day became cold enough to freeze the insulated mouthpiece hose of my hunter's camelback water bag. Always keeping at least a pocketknife and lighter in my pocket, I built a fire well removed and downwind from our best hunting area in order to thaw his water. Even with periodic access to a warm fire, it was a long day by the time we headed downhill in the gathering darkness as per my instructions. It was so dark by the time we got back down that I almost walked right past our horses, which would have been a serious disaster. Some guide I was turning out to be!

My unimpressive reputation didn't improve until two days later, when my important hunter, Les, shot the biggest bull elk anyone had seen in that country for several years. Suddenly, I went from zero to hero. To make it even better, there was a conflict with the other hunter.

Les was a military marksman and had made an incredible 370-yard shot, according to the range finder in his high dollar scope. I knew immediately it was a lung shot by the unmistakable *thump* of slug striking ribcage. The bull, however, was on a ridgeline above us and didn't drop but started walking away, disappearing from sight over the ridge. We were both excited and Les, a football coach, was anxious to run up this considerable mountain to finish off his elk. I calmed him down, telling him that with a lung shot it's best to hang tight and take your time. This allows the animal to lie down and bleed out rather than trying to run farther if they think they're being pursued. Right about then, we heard another series of three shots over the ridge, right where Les's elk had just disappeared. We both almost killed ourselves racing to the top of the ridge.

Cresting the ridgeline, we didn't see the bull or any other hunters but immediately found the blood trail. It was bright red (oxygenated) and bubbly to confirm that it had been a lung shot. I told Les to stay on the trail while I jogged ahead to see where the shots had come from. I soon came into sight of an orange vest on the next ridge. Heading that direction, I could make out the enormous rack of the dead elk next to a hunter. As I approached, the hunter sat sideways to me on a rock next to the elk. He didn't seem to want to look at me. I told him that my hunter had put a lethal shot into that bull and we'd been tracking it. He responded that the elk had been just fine when it ran past him. I seriously doubted this but knew the law favored the final shot that put the animal down.

I went over and waved Les up to the ridge. The other hunter still refused to face me and kept messing with his cell phone trying to call someone, but had no reception. As Les approached, the other hunter stood and unstrapped the revolver he'd been keeping his hand on. That was why he'd remained sideways to me.

Les faced the other hunter. "I put a lethal shot into that bull and we were tracking him."

"He looked just fine when he came through here," the other hunter reiterated.

"That's the first elk I've ever shot," Les pleaded.

"That's the first bull I ever shot," the hunter replied.

"I've got four hundred bucks in my pocket for you to just walk away," Les offered.

"It ain't about money! You know that!" the hunter countered.

Les was holding a custom, left-handed action, 308 Winchester rifle with a high-tech scope—all top of the line. "I'll give you four hundred and my rifle," he offered.

"It ain't about that!" the hunter sputtered.

"Well," Les said, "I shot it. I'm going to at least get a picture with it."

He handed me his iPhone and posed between the enormous horns.

After the photo, he reluctantly said, "Well, I guess we might as well go."

The other hunter had been acting pretty strangely ever since I'd shown up. He appeared to be unduly nervous about something. I knew something was up and I'd finally noticed, while taking the photo, that he hadn't tagged the bull yet. I silently motioned for Les to sit back down. We sat for several minutes without saying a thing. The hunter was about to jump out of his skin. He kept trying his cell phone.

After a long, uncomfortable silence, I said, "I don't see a tag on that bull." Les turned toward me with a slight smile. The hunter kept messing with his phone. He was starting to break a sweat in spite of the cold.

After another eternally long silence, I said, "It's starting to warm up a little. That bull needs to be gutted. I'm not leaving here till I see a tag on that bull." The hunter still refused to look at me but said to Les, "Show me the blood trail."

Les could hardly suppress his grin as he walked back along the blood trail, pointing it out to the hunter. Pretty soon, the hunter just walked away without looking back at me. Les came back grinning from ear to ear, carrying his rifle with his four hundred bucks still in his pocket.

The guy had almost certainly been "buddy hunting," which is obviously illegal. He must have had a cow tag and was trying desperately to call his friend with a bull tag. Les said the hunter had asked which way the road was, indicating not only that he was lost, but also that he'd come by ATV, which could have only come within several miles away from this location. He almost certainly would have just taken the rack and left the meat. We didn't feel any too bad about having chased him off!

Back at camp, as I prepared to head back with pack saddles to bring the elk down, Shawn held out a GPS to me and asked, "You any good with one of these?"

"I don't know. What is it?" I replied.

Shawn just shook his head. "Here, let me show you. You're going to need this to get that elk out."

"I know where that elk is better than that little black box does," I replied. "And I couldn't read that thing without reading glasses if I did know how to use it."

"If it's where you told me it is, you can't get there the way you're thinking you can," Shawn told me. "It gets really thick with scrub oak below that ridge, so you have to go around and drop in from above. Believe me, I've tried it before."

Now, this was a guy who'd been guiding and packing in this country for thirty years. I'd seen him lead overweight, inexperienced riders up dangerous, icy trails that I might have normally gotten off and walked my mule through. It would have been pretty dumb not to heed his advice. He had me take the GPS, warning that it was worth more than I was and told me to radio another guide, Glen, who was close to that area with his hunters, when I got close enough to make radio contact. I was to tell Glen it was imperative that he assist me with packing this elk (against the normal policy of guides packing their own hunter's kills) so he could show me a reasonable route to pack out.

I headed out with Les, his dad—another Les—and his son, Wyatt, who was too young to hunt but had come along from Tennessee just for the elk camp experience. When I got close enough to radio Glen, he informed me that the route Shawn had proposed was so covered with deadfall from a recent windstorm that it would take days of chainsawing to get a horse through. I decided to try to bushwhack the route that Shawn had so adamantly warned against, knowing that if we had any trouble, I might as well throw his GPS in the creek and just go home unemployed.

The route turned out to be manageable and I had the elk back to camp before dark of the same day it was shot—a decent accomplishment for even an easy packing job. We took photos of Les Jr., Les Sr., and Wyatt between the enormous horns—three generations of Elk Foundation funders almost certain to show up in *Bugle* magazine and such: an advertising dream come true for Shawn. I was redeemed for all my prior screw-ups and was suddenly the most requested guide. My honest confessions of having nothing to do with finding or shooting the elk were all assumed to be false modesty and the fact that this happened on my third day on the job in unfamiliar country only augmented my ill-deserved reputation as super guide. My newly bushwhacked trail became known as the Duke Mule Trail.

After several trips up to Paradise Lake and back, during which two horses had taken serious falls and another had come up stone-bruised while my mules did fine, Shawn himself finally came up to me one day and said, "Well, I guess them little mules of yours ain't so bad after all."

***

During my odd jobbing and trail guiding days, I'd also built another small log cabin on our place outside Carbondale, allowing us to move into it and rent out our larger cabin. This helped relieve our financial strain enough that Kathy could finally quit the job that she really despised by now. Finally feeling free, she announced that we would be packing the mules along the Colorado Trail during the upcoming summer. This is about a 500-mile trail from Denver to Durango, mostly above timberline, that she'd been talking about for years.

Unfortunately, Kathy's wonderful old molly mule, Rosey, whom we'd purchased to replace Sexy several years earlier, had formed a malignant tumor that eventually forced us to put her down. Although we'd only had her a few years, she'd worked with me as trail guide and hunting guide and had proven to be kind and gentle, yet large and strong, a completely reliable companion in any situation. We hated to lose her and I was especially saddened that she wouldn't be with us on this grand adventure.

It was February when we decided to get serious about finding Kathy a new animal soon enough to have time for them to get to know each other and feel confident on the trail. We went to the horse sale at the Montrose auction yard, mainly to get educated and get a feel for what might be available and what prices were. By now, I'd become a pretty good judge of critters and knew what sorts of traits and personalities I was looking for, but I'd promised Kathy I wouldn't bid on anything without talking to the owners, who often attended the sale of their horse for that reason. Being able to judge both the owner and the animal is the best way to know if the animal is well broke and gentle.

The February sale was often referred to as the "killer auction" because folks tended to get rid of their undesirable animals during late winter, when hay was expensive and the horse market poor. The dog food market buyers always attended the February sale.

At the auction barn we ran into a good friend and experienced horseman, Jeff. Jeff had been raised in a family that had traditionally bred and trained horses for the ranching community in the Roaring Fork Valley. He'd used to ride herd during summers for the cattlemen's association, packing salt and tending cattle while breaking about twenty young horses on the job. He would have a sale after fall round-up every year at the local rodeo grounds, and his horses were very popular and brought top dollar. Now, he was an outfitter and kept about a hundred and fifty horses that he used and rented to other outfitters and stables.

There were several mules at the sale, and Jeff bought a couple of them that I'd been interested in. One looked just like Rosey and was so tame that the sales assistant running animals through the ring jumped on her over her rump, Lone Ranger style, turned around backward, rode her around the arena without a headstall or bridle, and then did a backward somersault off her and crawled under her belly. I called Jeff the next day and he agreed to sell her to me. I'd loaned him my Cacaloco dump truck a few months earlier to haul manure and he was glad to return a favor.

When I got to Jeff's pasture to find the molly and see if I could catch her in a several hundred-acre pasture, she was accompanied by a young line-back dun mare who really caught my eye. She was a beauty I'd noticed going through the sale ring, but I'd judged her to be a wild two-year-old as she bucked and kicked through the ring. Now I could see she was a bit older than I'd thought and was much calmer. She actually chose me more than vice versa. She danced up in a high-stepping trot with tail high and head tucked in before slowing down to approach and sniff me, head to toe, in introduction.

The mule was pretty nice, too, but only pretty nice, and quite a bit older than I'd thought. The mare's hooves still bore the nail holes of having been shod, which is often an indicator of being broke. I was sure Jeff had bought her for re-sale because she was too light boned and delicate to pack around fat Americans and other big game. All the outfitter and stable horses had to be large and stout and were often bred from drafters. I called to asked him about the mare. He thought I was kidding. I had a reputation as being strictly a mule guy and nobody had seen me with a horse before, although I'd owned a few over thirty years earlier. After a little necessary razzing about my change of heart, Jeff agreed to sell her.

Honey, as we named her, turned out to be a total dream! She was gentle and better trained than anything I'd ever had before. She loved people and loved to go riding. She turned out to be a registered Paso Fino, a gaited horse breed developed in South America from the original Spanish Barb stock that I was so partial toward. She loved to run and had endless endurance, able to run for miles, but she would also calm down quickly when asked to, which is pretty unusual. I'd had horses and mules before with that sort of speed and endurance, but such animals generally get so would up that they can't calm down and they tend to become unmanageable runaways.

You couldn't ask for a better, fast-walking, tough-footed, and enthusiastic friend for any sort of trail. We were as well mounted and well prepared for the Colorado Trail as possible.

Take a Hike, Old Man

The trail guide's creed: "Never let being lost take the fun out of not knowing where you are." Our Colorado Trail hike didn't start well. We got lost twice in the first half day. Well, three times if you count being lost before we even reached the trail head. The whole first week or so was a calamity of errors mostly having to do with my equines. The trail spirits were speaking, but I wasn't listening.

I wasn't looking for any kind of spiritual, self-improvement type of journey. Sure, I figured that missing several dozen happy hours at all my favorite hangouts wouldn't do me any harm, and I was hoping to get in better shape and maybe clear my head a little. But as far as "climbing the mountain" seeking knowledge, enlightenment, self-awareness, or any Paulo Coelho variety of spiritual quest, I'm too much of a cynical, smartass cowboy type to buy into that sort of happy horseshit. But as so often in life, I found everything I wasn't looking for and didn't think I needed.

First day, we took a wrong turn in a bad lightning storm and went backward a few miles. Second day, Paco, our mini Aussie shepherd with thousands of miles following equines, got stepped on seriously by Kathy's mare but was still able to travel. That night, we discovered my sleeping bag had fallen out of a pannier and I spent a cold night in a bivy bag at 10,500 ft. before backtracking seven miles and dropping

2,000 ft. to retrieve it. Third evening, I'd left my electric fence line at the previous camp and backtracked ten miles to retrieve it. This screw up, however, was a blessing in disguise as the backtrack was through a beautiful, six-mile-long meadow riding Kathy's gaited Paso Fino, Honey, with my mule, Zeb, and donkey, Lucky, running loose alongside bucking and kicking. Honey wanted to run, and I put the reins down and let her go, steering only with my legs and weight, dodging and jumping shrubby cinquefoil past elk and moose in the meadow and feeling like part of a wild herd.

It reminded me of the old days with my first mule, Fart Blossom. I'd started many mornings on desert camping trips with a several-mile wild ride with nothing on Blossom and wearing only my hat, skivvies, and tennis shoes while the rest of my herd ran bucking, kicking, and frolicking all around us. That is how I was dressed during my best ride ever up Courthouse Wash in Arches National Park with a bunch of pissed off park rangers and a posse of mounted volunteers in hot pursuit while my wild herd frolicked around us. They'd gotten in trouble. I don't know what for. I never asked.

Meanwhile, back on the CT, it was a great ride on Honey and a great stroll down memory lane and my glory days with Blossom, but it left me with the vague feeling of something missing. It took a couple more weeks of walking to realize that the missing thing was me.

Several days later, we walked into Gold Hill between Frisco and Breckenridge leading our animals due to cinch sores and stone bruises after just under 100 miles on the trail. As a wilderness and hunting guide, I'd traveled much harder country with heavier loads without any such problems and was baffled and frustrated. Having shifted loads mostly to Zeb, soft as silk but tough as nails, and having walked all the animals for several days, the equines were mostly recovered and ready, but we'd heard talk of avalanche remnants near Copper Mountain, so I arranged to trailer the critters home and switch to backpacks at least until we got past the snow debris. We trimmed our loads down to two backpacks weighing almost fifty pounds each and set out on foot late the next day.

We immediately ran into the Breck Epic, a 500-rider mountain bike race that we had to dodge all day and that would have been disastrous with the critters. We then encountered an avalanche field that could have been a death trap for equines. I began to concede that this wasn't a good year for equines on the CT, but it was still another week before I started listening to the trail.

We were trudging along under our heavy packs, carrying three weeks' provisions for ourselves and the dogs while learning that everyone else was carrying fifteen- to twenty-pound packs of lightweight, high tech stuff and resupplying every two or three days. We couldn't really change plans at that point and resolved ourselves to just moving more slowly than most and proud that we weren't hitting towns every few days. One day, talking to a young Canadian woman, I learned she was carrying about thirty pounds, almost the same percentage of her own weight I was carrying, and doing almost twice our distance daily. No big deal, she was much younger, and I was content to go easy and stop to catch my breath once in a while. That's when something snapped in me. Stop and catch my breath? Any athlete knows one doesn't stop and catch breath, athletes lead with breathing and they don't catch breath, they expel it. Hard!

It suddenly dawned on me that I hadn't gotten old, I'd just quit trying. I wasn't just trudging down a trail, I'd been trudging through life. Mid-sixties isn't that old. I'd just become lazy, resting on my laurels and leaning on excuses. Since when had I settled for being at the back of the pack? When had I forgotten how to breathe? Breathing is living! When had I forgotten how to live? Running runs in my family. My little brother, John, and I used to run fourteeners in pretty competitive time. My older brother, Bill, was a high school national champion runner.

Brother Bill, by the way, is now a local doctor in the Valley Urgent Care Center. That revealed, I'm compelled to provide the disclaimer that, other than being best of friends and having both been good runners, we are very different people. Let it suffice to say that it's a good thing that he's a doctor and I'm not. I don't know if he's also had his spiritual cage rattled lately. You might ask him next time you break an arm or need stitches. He's the nicest guy you could hope to meet and known to be very talkative and philosophical. He would be especially good to visit if you think you're dying. You would almost certainly live to talk about it and have someone there to talk about it with. The one stop doc.

Meanwhile, back on the CT, I was getting angry with myself and wanted to charge up the next hill and make myself suffer. I wanted to dig deep, feel the pain. I started uphill, breathing hard. I heard echoes of old coaches and senseis (teachers): "If you stop, you better be puking!" Soon, my feet found the rhythm of my breathing. I heard the roaring of my heartbeat in my ears, the rush of endorphins through my brain, but no pain.

I experienced a rush of thoughts and revelations, some good, some bad, while my brain rapidly sorted through keeping the positive and expelling the negative—like breathing. *Careful! Slow down! Something's gonna give! Reject, reject, reject. Harder! You can do it! LIVE YOUNG OR DIE! Keeper, keeper, DOUBLE KEEPER!* I pushed harder, wanting to struggle for reserves and willpower. Instead, I kept feeling better. It all felt very familiar and good, like coming home.

As a Gemini, can I claim to have had a self-reunion? That's what it felt like. Suddenly, I was at the top of the hill, my head roaring like a wild coastline. I'd never felt so alive! I knew then why my equines hadn't been invited on this journey. It had to be me, all me, and only me. It was as though all the best of me had to be called in to expel all the worst of me. A long time in coming, but as simple as breathing.

It took a couple days for my old body to catch up with my new attitude, but my optimism and energies kept increasing. My heavy pack was no longer an excuse, but felt like necessary ballast to keep me from floating away. I was loving the trail, but anxious to finish in order to pursue other goals. I'd never felt so enthusiastic about everything. We had a resupply planned for Cottonwood pass in a couple days, but I was so into hiking that I almost dreaded the interruption, even for a cheeseburger.

The resupply was being provided by my old friend, Steve Jackson, once again entering into this book. He has entered, or provided, many of the adventures of my life. When he was writing his book on the Chris Klug story, *To The Edge and Back*, about Aspen's own home-grown hero who survived a liver transplant and recovered to become the first U.S. Olympic snowboard medalist, Jackson had invited me along on the U.S. snowboard team European tour as their official photographer. Everyone knew I wasn't a real photographer and that Jackson had only brought me along as a drinking buddy, but they also thought that with a foolproof digital camera, even someone as dumb as a dipstick would get at least a few good photos. They were wrong. I didn't know cameras had a delay setting, nor did I know that one could scan through to view previous photos. I guess I figured that the tiny digital film would eventually go to some digital darkroom for digital developing. I wasn't invited back.

Meanwhile, back on the trail…

"Wait a minute. What's going on?" a reader might ask by now. "Isn't this chapter supposed to be about the Colorado Trail? Why all the wandering narrative? What's the point in all this?"

Well, far better writers (not to mention better photographers) have failed to capture the magnificent beauty of the Rocky Mountain high country, so why waste anyone's time on that effort? And how does one aptly describe the way a forest can wake up buzzing, literally, with the sound of countless unseen insects busy starting their day while the frost still lay thick on the meadow? Or the bright and cheery song of an unknown bird in the dead of a cold, dark night?

I must stick to the telling of simpler stories that I can better comprehend and relate. And the wandering, distracted discourse? Most guys, and especially us jokers, will talk about anything and everything on earth before we'll consider discussing even the most remote possibility that we might be suffering from depression.

We did eventually wander into Durango, but this had long ceased to be any goal of great consequence for me. It's always the journey, not the destination. Sometimes one must walk a long way to appreciate the insignificance of distance. Some of the most important things in life are independent of time and space. The CT had put me on a path back to myself—a path with no unit of measure nor schedule.

So, here's the short version: I went for a long hike with a tired old man I thought was me. But I left him behind on a steep hill deep in the woods and returned feeling young, vigorous, and invincible. If ever the old guy sneaks up on me again, I'll take him for another long hike and leave him in my dust as far away as possible.

When the time comes that my body is too old and tired to outrun the old man, I'll leave it behind in the dust, too, along with the old man and, thus unburdened, I'll charge up that highest of all mountains that renders us all ageless and invincible. And there I'll find Blossom and Gunther and Sexy and Bo, and all the other critters I've known and loved—and we will all run together!

***

We still have Zebadiah, Honey, and Lucky, and we ride five to ten miles several times a week. We've moved to the Four Corners region of Colorado with the best of desert and canyonlands nearby to the west and the best of the high alpine even closer to the north and east. We have plans to hike most of the Colorado Trail backward (south to north) this summer, and we'll continue exploring the Four Corners region on extended pack trips with all our critters. We feel like we've discovered heaven on earth! While this is definitely not the end of our story, it's certainly a happy ending to our story so far.

Acknowledgements

I would like to thank Steve Jackson for cajoling and harassing me into putting this book together while mentoring me toward whatever feeble writing skills I have acquired. The greatest thanks to my wife, Kathy, without who's mandate for travel I would never have seen Tibet, Madagascar, Patagonia, and many fourteen-thousand-foot peaks, and to my daughters, Ellie and Emma, who not only survived but enjoyed the wild adventures I subjected them to, and then went on to surpass them and take them to the next level. Also, to a few special friends, T.J Russell, Brian Pettit, and Jim Walker, all of whom have initiated and enhanced many of the best times of my life, and to my many four-legged friends who have enriched my life beyond description.

For More News About Jim Duke,
Signup For Our Newsletter:

http://wbp.bz/newsletter

Word-of-mouth is critical to an author's long-term success. If you appreciated this book please leave a review on the Amazon sales page:

http://wbp.bz/donkeys

Visit the author's website at:
https://authorjimduke.com

Read his blog at:
https://wbp.bz/DukeBlog

Made in the USA
Las Vegas, NV
01 December 2023

81944305R00144